BELIEVE, ACT, LEAD

Your Journey to Success, Wealth, and Making an Impact

DR. HYND BOUHIA

Red Thread Publishing

Write to info@redthreadbooks.com if you are interested in publishing with Red Thread Publishing. Learn more about publications or foreign rights acquisitions of our catalog of books: www.redthreadbooks.com

Paperback ISBN : 978-1-955683-22-7

Ebook ISBN : 978-1-955683-23-4

Cover Design: Jaime Moncayo

Contents

*For every woman to **Believe** in herself and in her dream,*

__Act__ on it by doing the work strategically while embracing excellence through her genius and the value she provides,

*and Become a great **Lead**er by creating wealth and making an impact.*

Introduction

This year I turn fifty.

My four children still think I am thirty-nine. I kept the blur around my age for all those years. However, now they will know it for sure. They probably figured that out on their own, but still, they play along with me. My boy is fifteen and he is absorbing everything, while the three girls are lucky to be in a time where everything is possible with so many role models of women becoming great leaders around them.

This age milestone made me feel like celebrating the whole year just like a star. I was inspired by Jennifer Lopez, who announced a world tour and made it a summer-long birthday celebration. I was so much in the vibes of a summer celebration that I found myself celebrating Walt Disney World's fiftieth anniversary for the whole week. Wherever I went, I found a party with the number fifty on the balloons. I was in alignment with the vibes of celebrations. I was so focused on it, that all the energy went to that. Isn't that what we want more of? A life of celebrations and joy. Finding a reason to celebrate, imagine, and believe in a life of overflow and abundance. Getting yourself overwhelmed with those feelings that everything becomes so good and everything goes the way you are open to receive. Be so open that you can feel the overflow already in your hand. Trust the process and the harmony of the universe and the divine. The process will always make the how to go from one point to another unfold at the right time. Dots do not connect forward, they connect backward. It will always be beyond your own capacity and your ability to manufacture the how to get to your dream life.

I am just getting started.

I have an overwhelming feeling of having finally reached a point where I can be the business woman, the mathematician, the economist, the financier, the environmentalist, the strategist, the professor, the musician, the mother, the wife, the champion, the guide, the voice, the friend … *and* the mentor. Including all of my identities together and finding harmony in everything I do.

What I feel today is that I'm just starting to understand who I am and what I'm here to do and to create. This very journey started when I felt that calling to embark on the mission to empower a billion girls and women to grow confident, resilient, tech-savvy, and financially free. It's the cumulation of many experiences, joyful moments and achievements, and difficulties and challenges that helped me realize how I am destined to make a difference in the lives of women and thrive for success to show others what is possible.

Being petite, I've always looked younger than my real age. In the beginning, as I was starting my professional career, it was annoying. I constantly tried to look older by dressing up with a sharp suit and glasses to make me appear super intellectual and add some years. It didn't change anything. I still looked young, was considered young, and dismissed for being young, or at least that was what I was feeling at that moment.

But it was okay. What I knew best was to be excellent in my work, in my analysis, in my papers, and in any project I undertook. I chose excellence to be my brand since I was very young.

Even though my mum made sure that we went to bed, I felt the need to wake up in the middle of the night, while everyone was sleeping. I sat in the corridor outside of my room—which I shared with my sister, Mouna, who's one year older than me—and worked on math exercises and reviewed equations and theorems from physics.

In the morning, I was ready to be the best in the classroom. I did that over and over again. Despite all the odds, I made it to the top of the national exam in math and science, which helped me go to one of the best engineering schools in France.

I grew up in Morocco, in a family where traditions wouldn't allow girls to go study abroad. They settled down and got married. However, I did not have that inside of me. I felt I had the intellectual capacity to be an engineer, like my father, and to be in the male-dominated business arenas. I knew deep inside that my only way out was excellence! This was the only aspect of my life I had control over. It was scientific. If you studied and worked hard, your grades would show it. The proof was there.

In those years of studying, of sitting in the best universities in the world —from Harvard to John Hopkins to Oxford—and having the most exclusive jobs—at the World Bank, in the Prime Minister's office, and at the Stock Exchange—so many important things happened to me and all of them led me to where I am today.

My whole life, I have been working hard, seeking excellence, to give my best in whatever I was doing. As a daughter, as a sister, as a student, as a graduate, as a researcher, as a professor, as an executive, as a professional, as a wife, and as a mother.

Wearing different hats, juggling different roles, keeping the smile, keeping the faith, and believing always in a better future for me, for you, for all of us.

I knew early on that I had a role to play. A role bigger than myself, transcending frontiers and barriers.

My role was to pave the way for young girls, for young women, and to show them what is possible. My role was always to stand tall in a very man-dominated environment, in meetings where I was the only woman. In strategy meetings chaired by the Prime Minister and Ministers, or the World Bank during weekly meetings chaired by the Vice President and the Directors who were all men—except for a Turkish woman who is in charge of the legal aspects. I was the special assistant to the World Bank Vice President of the Middle East and North Africa region. In that role,

I was in charge of monitoring the advances of the different projects and initiatives in the region. I was always the youngest in all those setups. Regardless, I knew that I had the knowledge deep inside of me, I had the expertise. And if I was missing something, I knew how to go get it from the best. I knew how to ask for help or mentorship whenever needed because I was embracing the journey as a quest for knowledge, experience, and evolution. I also understood that mentors would always be ready to help someone who was showing that she or he cared and was truly making all the efforts.

Knowledge boosted my confidence so profoundly that nothing could possibly shake it. Well, not always. I did have episodes of extreme vulnerability, and of feeling overwhelmed by responsibilities, challenges, and struggles. Plus, I was carrying so many responsibilities and such guilt from standing against what traditions dictated, not to mention I always felt like I needed to please everyone around me in order to be appreciated.

We come from a heavy culture and traditions which are anchored in women giving, and taking from yourself to give to others, because that is when you can attract goodness. I understand the concept of giving differently today. After having gone through so many experiences, not to mention my own pain and hurt, it took me a lot of searching within me and understanding the energy of giving and receiving to break free from the cycle and create a breakthrough for women to help them navigate with grace through their own lives.

I knew that my calling was beyond making myself happy with my work and my contribution, it was **to become a catalyst for every woman to grow confident, resilient, tech-savvy, and financially free**. I embraced this noble and empowering mission to be my full-hearted context for being, working, and persevering.

I came to self-development and transformation because I needed one at the lowest time in my professional career. I was already a mother of four, and I was pushing myself more than I could handle. I was pleasing everyone to get recognition and feel accepted and appreciated. Although my company was making seven figures and beyond, I cared the same way, or even more. As I attracted betrayal, losses, disappointments, and storms as an entrepreneur and a manager, I reached rock bottom. A few months before Covid hit, dressed in an elegant corporate suit, I had a board meeting for one of my companies where the tension and the conflicts were becoming overwhelming. Despite trying everything to stay calm and poised, this time I couldn't find my voice to speak, let alone holding on to any positive outlook. I felt that the whole world was attacking me and against anything I could say. As a CEO, all the responsibilities dropped on me and I took them. I knew that it was going to be tough. I stopped the activity, closed off the business, and absorbed all the losses. I paid off every investor with interests. Everything collapsed on my head. It was so dark. I went deep down financially, psychologically, and emotionally. I wasn't sure I could actually make it back.

Nevertheless, the story is that I didn't give up. I felt the unconditional love of my children and I knew I had to fight my own darkness. My whole system had to be rewired! This is how my journey today is about finding the light, finding the love, finding the courage, and finding the will to carry on and not give up no matter what.

I deepened my understanding and my ability to rise back up after having been crushed by the weight of responsibilities and difficulties. I want every woman in the world to do the same. I want every woman in the world to not be afraid of trying and persevering in her journey to reach success, create wealth, and make an impact.

So this became my calling from the moment I felt the change. I witnessed how the smallest light of hope can grow to overwhelm you and surround you with love, happiness, joy, and peace of mind. I started loving myself again after having gone through moments where I called myself hateful names. Having wrongly felt that I brought this to myself and that I was ashamed and that everyone was pointing the finger at me.

I have come a long way. Even writing about it wasn't possible for me at that time, because I was carrying too much rage and too many grudges within me. And I knew that stories do not help when they are shared from the open wound. It's when they are told from the scar that we can be inspired. It is from the scar that we can transmit empowerment. It takes such a deep and profound understanding of who we really are and elevates us to connect with the bigger power and the spiritual side.

Because there is a spiritual perfection in you. The moment you elevate to understand it and tap into it, it will help you rise. You will let go of any rage, any hatred. It all dissipates as you find the light. That is the spark I will share with you throughout this book.

The day I started seeing the innocence in all that happened to me and in the people whom I felt did me wrong at that moment, something deep inside of me shifted forever. And that shift wasn't physical, not logical, it was spiritual. This is the journey I'm taking you through in this book.

From that drive, I created the BAL Method, which stands for Believing in yourself and in the possibilities, Acting on it by getting the skills to be the CEO of your life and of your business, and becoming a Leader by making a true impact. It all stands on the understanding of your emotional intelligence and your awareness when it comes to all your feelings and emotions.

This method integrates my twenty years of experience as a strategist, financier, economist, consultant, and business owner. All the knowledge and the teaching in different universities and the mentoring brought me to where I am today and to create this incredible method to help women create wealth, reach success in their lives and their business, and make a truly sustainable impact.

Running businesses while caring for what we leave behind for the next generation has been my drive. Technically, sustainability integrates the three important aspects: economics, environment, and society. Three pillars to ensure that sustainability is included in everything we do—from industrial production, business development, services, entertainment, sports, culture, trade, politics, etc.

I always believed in the importance of integrating the future generations in the way business was being conducted and in setting up a long-term vision for everything we do. So making an impact was embedded in every action, every job I had, and during my entrepreneurship journey.

Integrating sustainability into business required a deep paradigm shift in the way businesses were approached and the way organizations handled profit maximization and social responsibility. Long meetings and conferences are organized continuously to raise awareness, give incentives, and to prove to everyone that business cannot be done the way it used to be. The business has a responsibility to protect the planet, to protect nature, to protect us. That is not just for business, it is a role we all need to play, by being responsible for ourselves and how we care for everyone around us through the legacy we leave behind.

Looking back, I realize I was instrumental in that big machine that drives the world and the sustainability paradigm and it made me feel good. Then I continued my mission by creating my own stage to carry my voice and to contribute to that paradigm by helping women become leaders for themselves and for the betterment of themselves, their families, and the world around them.

Within those celebratory vibes, the summer vibes, and looking after my four children during their summer vacation, I wrote this book. I'm filled with gratitude for how I was able to recreate myself these past two years and embody my mission as a catalyst for women's empowerment and leadership. And I want you to have that same feeling while reading it and appreciating every part of it as it resonates with your own life.

Use this book to ignite that drive in you to help you design a better life for yourself, to find the courage and the inspiration to carry on. From a space of love and caring, you can unleash the incredible force you have inside of you and bring magic in your life. Each chapter builds to the next one.

Becoming a leader is about leading yourself first. For that, there are a set of codes for self-leadership which I have compiled by working with women from all around the world and from different levels of education and industries. A whole future book will be dedicated to that.

This book is for you to believe in yourself and in all the possibilities, take actions and do the work by tapping into your genius and reaching excellence, and lead yourself to greatness.

Thriving and doing good at the same time is for me, for you, and for all of us.

A Journey of Leadership

My own leadership story started in my family's living room in Casablanca, where my professors convinced my parents to enroll me in the top engineering school in France, instead of staying in my home country, going to the local engineering school, and getting married, so that I could conform with the traditional route for Moroccan daughters during the eighties and early nineties. Things have changed now of course. I knew leaving Morocco would come with many challenges, including the personal pressure I felt for not conforming to my culture's expectations. However, I left for France believing in my grandmother's words. She told me that I could create my own life, one beyond the restrictions laid out for me. It's not that I didn't care about my family's wishes, but I knew I would be a better daughter, friend, and human following my own path.

During my doctoral studies at Harvard, and later on at Johns Hopkins, even during my stint working at the World Bank, my grandmother's words of encouragement kept me focused on what I could achieve. This was the beginning of my global life. I sought excellence in whatever I did. I worked harder, longer hours, and proved to myself every day that university was the right decision. Even when my male peers criticized me, saying women were too soft or too weak to make it in the business world, I was determined to honor myself and develop the needed skills to make the business a welcoming place for women.

When I was at Harvard working on my PhD thesis, I took the first courses that ever thought about evaluating the impact on the environment and integrating this new way of assessing business and doing business. It was the start of sustainable development. The whole notion was new in the mid-nineties. So, it became my calling to pursue sustainability in every part of business and to relate to everyone.

I made that my drive, my mission, and my context in everything I did. I became an expert and a reference in integrating sustainable development in policy-making, strategic planning, and business portfolios. I made it my objective to master how to optimize water management, integrate renewable energies, and creative industries and businesses that are very considerate of the water-energy-food nexus.

I started embodying this mission of sustainability and creating a better life for people around the world. As a young professional at the World Bank, it was possible to rotate for two years before settling down in a region, so I spent eight years traveling the world from Latin America, to Asia, to the Middle East and Africa. I was on a mission deeply anchored in development, sustainability, and a world free of poverty.

As I was fascinated by traveling and discovering new countries, I worked in regions I have never been to with the objective to discover different cultures, interests, and horizons. I started by working in Latin America focusing on Brazil, Argentina, and also the Caribbean, setting strategies for the environment and water infrastructure. Then I moved to South East Asia where I worked on poverty reduction in Laos, and a water infrastructure project in Thailand. My work took me to visit all the countries of the Middle East and North Africa with the Vice President of the World Bank. When I joined the World Bank Treasury, I worked on structuring bonds in emerging market currencies. It was another spree of traveling and discovering the biggest financial centers of the world and understanding how the financial system works and runs.

This period of my life was the most enjoyable. The hours were long, but it was worth it to be jet-setting around the world. I was particularly connected with the zen vibes of yoga and meditation. I had turned vegetarian for a couple of years during that time as I was getting more and more sensitive about the importance of eating healthy and of integrating yoga and meditation in my morning routine. My work at the World Bank took me to Thailand, Malaysia, Laos, and other countries in SouthEast Asia, and I was very sensitive to vibes and energy around meditation and some of the rituals in buddhism that brought a deep feeling of calmness and zen. In my missions to Thailand, I used to wake up with the sunrise. I felt focused and energized early in the morning. I would go to the yoga facility for Vinyasa and Ashtanga Yoga on the wooden structure by the river, close to a monastery so we could smell the scent of the amber wood and orchids. It's a scenery I go back to when I look for calmness inside of me. I found it there!

This was part of creating a new paradigm for the way business has been conducted, the way policies are being structured and strategies are being defined. A paradigm of service for a better future for everyone.

Find the Balance in Your Life

I never disconnected my work from my daily occupations and my role as a mother. They have been intertwined in every way. I took my children when I had to go on a business trip. My son, Dawud, went with me to Stockholm and attended the conference opening function when he was eight months old, and my then eighteen month old, Sarah, was the star of the African CEO Forum in Geneva, where I was a speaker. They were with me and around me as I was preparing projects, making speeches, and conducting meetings. I had birthday parties and events to go to, while connecting for meetings.

I left a meeting to go see my eight-year-old daughter's piano recital dressed in a suit with my high heels, rushing in but excited to have made it on time. My daughter, Joudy Noor, had such a beautiful playing on the piano with the full queue. It reminded me of my own piano lessons and competitions. I played piano for fourteen years when I was growing up. It was how I found balance in my life.

Piano brought me joy and elegance in my life. Chopin, Bach, Beethoven made me dream in the middle of the day and while learning history and geography lessons. Music kept me feeling good throughout the day. Now that I understand and work with energetics, I realize I maintained high vibes despite the competition, the homework, the exams. I appreciated the beauty of classical piano; it was liberating and the most beautiful relief. And when the music comes from your fingers you feel the intensity of it even more.

Ballet dancing and sports were my other activities growing up. I let go of them as things got more intense when I turned sixteen, but I never let go of playing piano. It was my identity. While having breakfast in the morning, I would sit and play a piece. I loved "Moonlight" by Debussy or the Nocturnes by Chopin. It was that perfect romance in my life and that grace that celebrated the feminine energy. Then I stood back up, put my shoes on, sat at my desk, and followed the most intensive plan for review to be in charge of all my lessons. The balance was well defined.

Throughout the years, that balance got shaky with the responsibilities, but today I see such a need for it to stand back up after a professional challenge. I speak for the importance of making that balance your normal way of being when you are alone with yourself and there is no obligation.

I found the balance through the love and the fulfillment of educating my children and developing a beautiful relationship with them, so that our ride together is the best they can ever want to have.

I didn't know how to be aligned with that harmony before. Luckily, it reached that as I deepened my understanding of mindset. I remember when I was pregnant with my youngest daughter and I had just started my new impact-focused advisory firm. I was helping several corporations and institutions define their sustainable development strategies as part of the preparation for the COP22.

However, I was hiding my baby under big scarves to avoid comments from male counterparts or anyone else in meetings or large ministerial gatherings. Because I was used to avoiding anything that reminded my clients and colleagues that I was actually a woman! I also thought I was too old to have a baby at forty-four when that's a beautiful miracle that should be celebrated everyday.

In reality, being a woman has never been the obstacle, it's more how we limit ourselves because of our own beliefs!

So, I chaired the ministerial meeting for the Water Day at COP22 and it was a great success. Then I realized that I didn't have to go through all the trouble of hiding my real self.

This is why it's vital to focus on overcoming the invisible constraint we all carry with us as accomplished, professional women. Because empowerment starts from within and what we choose to believe. Every woman deserves to be fulfilled both in her professional and personal life by finding the balance that's in line with who you really are.

The first thing I teach women just like you is to honor their womanhood and show up with confidence and power to gain notoriety with their leadership style.

After a full year of work and having helped more than a hundred women change their life, by attracting more wealth through new contracts, new jobs doubling their salaries, launching new projects and new programs, I want to celebrate with all the gratitude for being part of this co-creation. I wanted to feel happy and enchanted, so the whole trip to Disney World unfolded. There were many ups and downs with setting the travel after the pandemic and the lockdown. Then, I found myself walking with my four children inside of the incredible magic of Walt Disney World.

I was still connecting and working. I knew I would be missing a conference about empowering women through technology as I wouldn't physically be there but it was okay. I was the master of juggling many things at the same time. Yet this time it felt different. I didn't have that sense of guilt that was always hanging over my head. I was freed from the shame you carry when you go through what people perceive as failure, because we worry too much about what others think. And when you start realizing that what people say about you, and what people think about you, is not your business, you feel light suddenly. Life became lighter, almost too silent from what I was used to. And that's the normal way of being.

On a perfect day, we were walking under the impressive Space Sphere in EPCOT at Walt Disney World. I was happy to see my four children discovering so many things, and having access to simplified concepts about space and rocket science.

At the same time, I was scanning the area, looking for a place to sit to connect and speak at the conference happening in Morocco that very morning. A special event about "building tomorrow's global workforce" was starting that same day, and I was in the program to speak at the special roundtable about empowering women through science and technology. I was on stage with two incredible female American astronauts, the head of the Space Foundation, and a high-level gathering of participants. We were all ready to discuss how to empower women through science and technology.

The world had gone digital and technology was moving at the speed of light! And all this was calling for the mastering of advanced technologies for every young girl and young woman, so they could have a place in the economy and in their community.

So, I connected from under the big Sphere in EPCOT. I was focused. I felt like I was there, just as if I were sitting at the conference with those incredible women leaders. The discussion was incredible, and technology made it possible. Ah, to be in those two places at the same time and feel good about it!

Not just technology, but living with a deep trust for things to work out no matter what. Having the faith about how life's unfolding the way you want it to be. Faith is actually having trust without any evidence of it. Yes, possible. Just like a young woman could dream of becoming an astronaut, and she made it happen. Or another young woman wanted to become a space expert and she did. All possible, when you believed, you held on to your dream, and you remembered who you are and what you valued most.

My message at the conference was for every young girl and every young woman to dream big. To never let anyone or anything dismiss it, and to choose excellence as your brand.

What makes all of this possible is finding your balance, holding on to it when you find it, and using it as your point of reference. Just like this very conference. I was supposed to be there, but my family trip got confirmed at the same time. Being a full-time professional and a full-time mother, my life mirrors the balance between the two. That day was exactly about what that balance meant for me and the way we strive to make it happen.

For me, this balance is being a mum and knowing that I'm doing a great job raising my four children. Being a professional and knowing that I care so much for my clients, for the empowered leaders in my Masterminds, and for my connections. Embracing my mission to empower a billion girls and women to grow confident, resilient, tech-savvy, and financially free.

This is why you need to stand strong and unshakable on top of a triad of three beliefs for you to make it all work. The belief in yourself. The belief in your work and your profound mission. The belief in your connections, your clients and your partners and whoever matters for your work and your personal life.

Get those vibes in by integrating into your morning routine a brief moment and see how you can strengthen each part of this triad every day. Embrace and trust the balance that makes sense for you most in your life.

Celebrate in The Name of Gratitude

When we celebrate, it's a way for us to express joy and happiness. Celebration becomes a ritual when you throw it in the name of gratitude.

Being grateful is about honoring yourself and honoring what you have in life, as small as it may be. You cannot possibly conceive the path of your life better than what unfolds for you. This is why we hear over and over in the self-development world "life is happening for you and not to you." Things, events, and situations are happening to carry you from one level to another, from one dimension to another. No matter how they feel at the moment, with time you will come to understand that they happened to strengthen you and to bring you more power.

The way I picture it in my mind is different circles. Each circle holds the thoughts, the feelings, the actions, and all the doing ... and therefore the results. If you want to see your results changing, you need to change your circle to a higher one. You cannot change your results by keeping the same bitterness about what you have. Your feelings, your thoughts, everything has to change. And the only way to change that is by being deeply and profoundly grateful for what you have. Things you have taken for granted in your life. The fact that you can sleep in a comfortable bed and wake up in the morning and smell the freshness of the day. You can walk outside and feel the sun burning your skin. This is enough to make you breathe life and focus on the joy of what nature gives with abundance. Just that feeling is overwhelming when you focus on it and be present in the moment. What makes us feel lost is living too much in the past, or focusing on an invisible future you don't want to see happening.

When you bring yourself back to the present and you focus on your senses and your feelings, you can truly be in the moment. Just like you would reboot your phone when it's stuck and you don't know what to do. You switch it off and put it back on. That's it. If things aren't going the way you want them—when you lose control of yourself, your thoughts, your feelings, your life—instead of stimulating yourself in the wrong direction and amplifying all the negativity that comes from the stress, the fear, and the doubt, let go of all the energy that is not helping you. The negative energy that brings you more resentment, rage, or anger. Give up the idea that the past could have been better or the desire for people to be the way you want them to be. Let go.

Pushing the reset button is coming back to the present moment, grounding yourself through yourself. Creating a safe bubble for you by opening your awareness about your thoughts and the voice inside of your head.

When you say to yourself that you're not good enough, you are telling the world that you need help. You can grasp it in two different ways. The first way comes from your manipulative side, so your call is to receive praise and to hear that you are great. This means that your doubt is so overwhelming you need continuous reassurance and feeling safe from the outside world. That's the echo of something hurtful from your past or a voice you kept inside of you. The second way, and it is deeper, you're actually calling out for help from the universe, the divine, the cosmos. You're calling for help deep inside of you, because you know that you are destined for more. Referring to Michael Bernard Beckwith, asking for HELP is a prayer. Using the word as an acronym H.E.L.P, Beckwith explains it as: Hello Eternal Loving Presence. And HELP is a shorter version of that prayer.

Stop and take a moment to learn how to listen to your inner guidance. Your intuition is there. It's suffocated by the hurt, pain, and layers of negativity you have absorbed through the years.

To be able to connect with that, you need to put in place a spiritual practice. It can be meditation, praying, or reading religious texts. Find the spiritual practice that most fits with who you are. That's how you nurture yourself and how you feed your inner light for it to grow until it overwhelms you.

Within my path to enhancing my spiritual practice, I started a gratitude journal and every day I wrote down ten things I was grateful for. In the beginning, the list included basic things from the pillows I loved sleeping on, the flowers in my garden, and the tea I enjoyed in the morning. Then the list got more sophisticated with time. It has become my spiritual practice, leading me to a more peaceful and meaningful life. It helped me rise from one circle to another. My journey is still ongoing, and every day I celebrate the evolution and growth no matter how small it is. It made me feel in control of myself.

If you do the gratitude for twenty-one days, you will see something coming into your life as if by magic. You change your spiritual DNA by doing that. Clearing the clutter by refocusing on things that feed your soul. I see it in women who have participated in our masterminds and feel at times reluctant to do it. You need to take the time and actually do the gratitude. It's not the thinking of it that will help you, it is the doing of it. Those feelings and the spiritual connections that come from it will strengthen your power. And then you trust in universal harmony. You understand that whatever is meant for you will come to you. Even if you don't see the evidence, you continue on believing. As you surrender to the possibilities, you'll start appreciating every moment of life. You will find the beauty in you, the perfect in you. You will honor the glory inside of you.

I wouldn't be who I am without my stories. Even though I hated some of the toughest moments I have gone through, they made me discover a dimension I never understood anything about.

It's not so much what you go through that makes you grow, but how you go through it. When you honor every moment, by being fully present, you will find gratitude in every step. By holding on to it, it grows. It amplifies and gives you the base and the foundation to carry on towards your desires and your dream.

Gratitude is saying yes to what you have and expecting more. Gratitude is being happy for what you have and feeling ready for more. Gratitude is saying thank you for the smallest thing and opening your arms for more.

When you celebrate who you are, that means that you honor yourself and you express gratitude. And providing a service comes from the realm of gratitude. For being able to serve, for finding the clients to serve, and for co-creating together better conditions. We grow together and we feed each other from those connections.

This is why my mission is to celebrate women in every sense of who they are and to have them feel that they are extraordinary, perfect, and so powerful in what they do and who they are. The world will be a better place when women are empowered, appreciated, and celebrated. We will all be better off.

Strive For a Big Mission

Many girls and women, especially in the developing world, need encouragement to reach for their true potential. This is why I utilized the skills I learned in my training to embark on a mission to empower one billion girls and women to grow confident, resilient, tech-savvy, and financially free.

We are living in an unprecedented era, where business seems to favor the rise of women in the spotlight. Women are stepping forward to share their gifts with others, leading with great service and sustainable impact. I asked myself how women in leadership are reflected in the daily realities of women's lives, and realized that women in leadership are not just for global superpowers or highly developed countries but are foundational to each girl and woman looking for examples of how to express their integral purpose in their communities.

After twenty years of experience in development, strategy, and finance, I connect leadership to the level of influence and impact in a community. They are intertwined in every way. **Leadership is to be able to influence someone's thoughts, feelings, emotions, and actions to empower and inspire positive change.** This is why every woman is born to be a leader. She has what it takes inside of her.

My drive today is to give world class programs to empower women to become great leaders by creating wealth and making an impact. Together, we are building a new paradigm of business and leadership for the next generation, so that every woman will feed her motivation and spark from her own experience. If it's good, fill yourself with gratitude. If it's not the way you want it to be, use it to grow your inner strength and amplify your emotional intelligence. A setback, a bump in the road is considered failure only when you let it be final because you quit.

This book is about how to lead yourself so that you can take yourself from where you are today to creating a different life and get yourself closer to your objectives.

Leadership is not about gaining authority and power for yourself alone. Leadership is about being able to show up in a way that also empowers your peers, your community, your clients, your team, and your family to grow with you.

When you truly and profoundly embody that understanding of leadership, it becomes a mission on its own. It represents the reason why you want to show up and share value from a space of service, of helping and giving. All of this should come with the emotional energy of caring, loving, and connecting.

This applies to everything you do—from your work, your offer, your service, your consulting expertise, or your managerial responsibilities to your family, your relationships, and your friends.

For business in particular, this will not only change the way you perceive business, but how you articulate your business model, and how you take on your day.

Integrating this definition of leadership will help you show up authentically.

You will be amazed by the level of connection you'll genuinely create, the level of followers you will attract; and how you'll become a magnet to clients, opportunities, and abundance.

Take a moment to think about your own definition of leadership as you read through the different chapters of the book. The way you are leading yourself is the way you will reach the goal-achieved you. You have it in you, let it guide you!

Make It a Happy Life

Some people think that you can only be fifty percent happy and fifty percent not. Others think that you can be happy all the time. And others don't even see why we are asking ourselves these philosophical questions.

What is sure is that your happiness doesn't depend on external circumstances, it's based on your own emotional maturity.

We are born happy beings. A baby's laughter is the most innocent and spontaneous thing. And then we add so many filters that cover and alter that inner feeling of happiness. So, happiness becomes based on the conditions and circumstances. We link happiness to material things. If I have this house, I will be happy. If I have a multiple-carat diamond ring, I will be happy. If I have this car, I will be happy. If I reach this level of money in the bank, I will be happy. If I have this bag, this watch, and the list goes on.

Happiness has nothing to do with the material things you hold in your hand. It's an emotional state inside of you. Being happy is what you choose to emotionally be. Which means that if something doesn't go the way you want it, the happiness is still there inside of you. If something goes as you want, you will feel happy and aligned with those vibes for it to continue and persist just like you deserve it.

Because it is an emotional state, the spiritual awareness will enhance it, by removing all the layers and filters that prevent you from seeing a new way of looking at happiness.

I understood my own spiritual maturity when I started noticing that feeling happy didn't depend on what I heard or received. I learned how to disconnect no matter what happened around me. It becomes a solid central state. If a plan doesn't work out, I don't like it, but it will not alter my emotional state. Even if it does for a moment, I have learned how to ground myself and bring myself back to the central state. What you learn with practice and consistency is to collapse the time of you being scattered and upset.

You reach that level of stability in your emotional state of happiness when you can see great potential in every circumstance. This is you stepping into the realm of infinite possibilities. There's an energy behind the different circumstances and conditions that we go through, and this energy is pushing you and helping you to continue in your path of a life of growth and evolution. Being in harmony with the universe is about surrender and alignment with the laws of the universe.

The laws of the universe are structured around different axioms and theorems. We're all familiar with the law of gravity: an apple falls from a tree, it will reach the ground because of gravity. Similarly, the law of polarity states that in everything, every matter, there are opposite parts:

the positive and the negative. This means that when you perceive the negative part of anything, there is a positive part linked to it. As you train yourself to see those two parts, you will not only mature consciously and spiritually, you will embrace everything that comes your way. You'll open your arms by becoming a grateful receiver—ready for the overflow and abundance from the divine, the universal light and what you can consider as the infinite intelligence.

You will start understanding that in every circumstance, there's an energy behind it pushing us to grow, to reach a new expression of ourselves. Thus, when you are faced with difficulties and you feel stuck, you know it shall pass. When you see that every road is blocked, every window is closed, it is in your mental being. This is when you allow yourself to feel stuck. Because in reality, there is nothing physically blocking you. It is a mental state.

Leila was a successful executive, balancing her growing professional responsibility with two teenagers at home and also being an influencer on social media. Then she started separating the spaces. She was a different person with different personalities to better fit each part of her life. When you switch to becoming a different person in each arena, that means that you are lying to yourself in one of the places. It creates blockages and frustrations and it makes you feel that something is missing. As we went through the first phase in the empowered Leaders Mastermind, she started understanding her real identity and worked on aligning her beliefs with the way she wanted to be respected and perceived by everyone. When you study the mind and the interaction between the conscious and the subconscious mind you will understand how to control your thinking and start shifting the paradigm that controls your attitude. Thus, by changing her attitude towards every facet of her life, attracting more opportunities and signing a deputy managing director job, her life improved in a way she could never imagine possible before. I saw it happening with women working in the most exclusive corporations including Goldman Sachs, Citigroup, McKinsey, Google, and also in their own businesses. Similar breakthroughs happen for women in the public sector, in the government, and in the military.

When you become aware of all the possibilities that present themselves and how you can access them when you don't see them, your happiness becomes unshakable, as if you have created a shield around your energy, making your inner state your own. This is the moment you will feel in charge.

We will not deny that there are struggles and difficulties that can be overwhelming. Grief from a loss of a family member. The difficulties of losing a job, a company going bankrupt, or a relationship being ruined. All of these are painful circumstances. However, when you protect your inner emotional state, you can recreate yourself and find the strength inside to carry on and not give up because of the overwhelming challenges and misfortune. You should never give up! You will automatically grasp the infinite possibilities that come with them and find fortune in what showed up initially as a misfortune. We grow better at it as we mature spiritually and emotionally.

Use Feedback to Vibe Forward

When you get stuck and life doesn't go as smoothly as you wanted the ride to be, take it as feedback. Feedback to change the road, to turn towards another direction. Feedback comes from life with events or circumstances, or from people. It makes you change direction. It makes you alter your plan.

There is always a bigger energy behind you, pushing you towards a greater expression of who you are, helping you discover new levels of abundance and joy in your life. When the struggle or misfortune is perceived from this angle, it helps you carry on no matter what. You can witness how you feed from the life force. You will rise like a phoenix from the ashes.

Feedback helps you learn how to pay attention to what's happening around you. Feedback can also be criticism from people. There might be people unhappy with your work or clients who aren't happy with what is happening around them. The more you mature emotionally, the more you can stay grounded and be less affected.

When you reach that level of spiritual maturity and energetic under-standing, you will demystify the fear of failure, rejection, and any setback.

It isn't about letting go of fear. It's more about being able to walk along-side the fear and create your dream life. You grow your ability to coexist with fear and feel good with it. Because the fear will never disappear. There's a fine line between the excitement of life and the stimulation from stress and fear. We need all those feelings to feel alive, to grow and feel the excitement.

The deepest fear that I see in women when they come to my world is related to rejection, either in a relationship or finding a new job. When you get caught up in the worry of rejection, it means that your worthi-ness has been altered. It's an alarm sign for you to reboot your inner software and reprogram it. It makes you lose your self-worth if you get more focused on what others are thinking than about yourself. Keep your focus on the evolution and the growth that you are creating and experiencing in your life and not on the hurdles and the setbacks. If you spend too much time thinking about what people are thinking about you, you disperse your energy into a space you will never understand. Instead, focus your attention on yourself and how you are handling your work and your self-development.

Let go of what others feel about you or think about you. Focus all your energy on you and your mission. Shift your focus. Think about what the divine and the universe think about you. As a perfect spiritual creation, there are no mistakes in being who you are. So, if there are unexplained episodes of misunderstanding and struggles, they're part of your journey.

When you worry about what others are thinking, you will get yourself into the spiral of pleasing everyone around you. And pleasing everyone will impact your self-worth and how you are valuing yourself.

As a multicultural woman, I know the diversity that comes from carrying several traditions and cultures is truly amazing and priceless. Speaking several languages, dressing up with colorful, traditional outfits, being in your element everywhere, appreciating different types of cuisines, music, styles, and habits will make anyone feel so versatile, special, and unique in whatever field. However, the burdens and the responsibilities which are linked with all of these diversities can be overwhelming and at times too heavy on your shoulders. It makes you feel responsible for everyone around you and you want to please them all the time. You tend to forget what it's like to receive anything because you have the "always here to give" label. What's worse is that it can even make you feel stuck in an invisible box created by your heritage and your multi-cultural background. You may feel suffocated, overwhelmed, and with no way out.

I know how it feels! I have been there, and I'm still probably there, but with my own roadmap to help me navigate through the cultures, the traditions, and the multifaceted background.

When you let go of the constraints you face in your culture, you will feel liberated and capable of creating the life you truly desire.

What you really want is to free yourself from all of the heavy weight. You'll feel liberated! You will breathe all the goodness of your multicultural life. As the star of your life, you can shape it the way you wanted. You can take a bit of your traditions and background, and mix it with the modernity that suits you best. You can set a new trend in your family and reshape traditions to better fit your perspectives.

Where Focus Goes, Energy Flows

As I learned the lessons from studying and understanding the energetics around us and the connection between the perfection of the soul and the thoughts that take over our mind, I became more aware of how we let our thoughts and energy shape our life. Then I focused all of my energy in implanting my mission and creating all the value I meant to have by helping women thrive as great leaders in their lives.

As an entrepreneur, as a strategic consultant, I was managing several companies and structures. One of my companies found itself in the middle of turmoil, and I had to make the painful decision to close it down and absorb all the losses. I did everything I could to pay off all the investors with interest and to contain it. It was a deep dent of multiple millions for me to carry. But more than that, it was a moment of so much stress, tension, judgment, and so many interpretations. It felt like my identity was stolen and that people started to define me with everything that I was not. In the press, in the gossip columns, in the behind-the-scenes discussions. I wasn't sure I could handle all of this or how I could survive it. All of my focus was going there and it made it feel like a downfall spiral.

In this worst moment of my professional career, I saw all the losses, the difficulties, and people pointing their fingers, and felt the hurt and the shame that comes with it. My mind was spinning around negative thoughts and taking me to a state of despair I had never visited before!

Doubt started to settle in. Self-esteem was gone for a ride.

You don't know what confidence means anymore. This is when you become indecisive. You try to look for answers and solutions everywhere. By reading books, or listening to motivational videos and podcasts. You're looking for that missing piece. You start asking everyone around you which way to go. The basic decisions seem so complicated to make. If you want to change your hairstyle, you need everyone's approval. And if you want to change the color of the walls in a room in your house, you can't choose on your own. What happens is that your boundaries drop and you let more people into your life. Which makes you even more confused, overwhelmed, and more in doubt.

After spinning around myself for so long, I discovered that the power comes from inside. Guidance comes from within you. And the only way to reverse your deceiving results is by taking charge of your mind and yourself. Stopping negative ideas can only happen when you start being grateful for the basic things you actually have in your life. Believe me, I know how hard that is when your problems and challenges feel bigger than yourself.

It's all about your energetics and the vibrations you find yourself aligned with. The more you express gratitude, the more you will manifest things to be grateful for, and you can steer away from the fear. Because fear and gratitude cannot coexist together in the same place. So, I will choose gratitude all the way.

The BAL Method

This is why I created the Believe-Act-Lead Method (BAL Method) to take you step by step to greatness. It is a well proven method—with many success stories—to help every woman become empowered and attract abundance and success in her life.

I was looking for an approach and a process to become your savior when you feel overwhelmed with life, with work, and you need that little something to reach the level of wealth and success you know you deserve. If you feel you have done everything and it's still not working, it is in the realm of mindset that you will find the key. And if you feel that you don't know what to do, it is both about mindset and strategy, and the secret lies in the right combination of both for you.

The first thing to do is to understand the importance of balance in your life and in everything you do.

The BAL Method is articulated around three phases to create a magical and lasting transformation. The first phase is about making you *believe* in yourself again and in your dream. The second phase is to *act* by mastering the strategic tools and access financial intelligence. And by the third phase, you know how to *lead*, become an empowered leader and an unstoppable entrepreneur, creating wealth and opportunity and building a lasting legacy with a sustainable impact.

After twenty years of experience in strategy and finance, I have condensed all my expertise and experience to design a thorough method to empower women and help them create wealth and make an impact. For that, I structure a three step method for every woman to Believe in her dream, Act on it, and Lead with it, using the Believe-Act-Lead Method (BAL Method).

The BAL Method helps reverse engineer what it takes to be an empowered and an empowering leader and a successful entrepreneur by becoming more confident in your decisions, more in tune with your purpose, and creating a life of financial freedom.

1. The first phase is to Believe in yourself and in the possibilities. Everything starts by knowing who you are. It's only then that you will be able to imagine and define your personal and professional goals. Your purpose will then find its way to you. This first part is essential to get the right mindset for success and great achievements.

2. The second phase is about taking Actions and structuring a clear strategic plan. Creating the life of your dream and becoming an empowered leader takes discipline and consistency. By acquiring the business skills, decision making schemes, and branding, you will get access to financial intelligence and build the foundation for success.

3. The third is about mastering how to Lead with your talents and gifts. This phase focuses on harnessing leadership skills. It also integrates the understanding of making an impact in the world and building your legacy through your business and your expertise.

This method gives you the foundation to structure a great offer based on the value you provide. By understanding the meaning of service, you can not only unlock the secret to wealth and fulfillment, but you will become a magnet, attracting amazing wins in your life.

Hundreds of women have mastered this method and attracted amazing wins and incredible changes in their lives, and this year we are reaching thousands.

These women have reclaimed their power, becoming leaders of their own lives and in control of what is happening to them. Julia was able to leave a job she never liked and started her own human resources consultancy when she boosted her self-image and connected with her inner strength. Julia is an example of how the phase one of Believe and mindset can change someone's life.

Sarah worked on her branding and positioning and started attracting premium clients for her copywriting business. This illustrates how, by acting and working on the branding and showing up as an authority in your market, you can attract more money in your business and that's phase two of the method about acting.

Judy found the right investor for her start-up operating in the clean energy space. As we got to phase three about leading, Judy embraced the leader in her, she leveled in her network, and found herself in the same rooms as high-level investors.

I love these examples because they illustrate how each phase covers different layers of transformation, crashing the glass ceiling and breaking free from any preconceived barrier. They humble me and inspire me to fine tune the method and make it more crisp and adaptable to the incredible diversity that women bring.

I'm celebrating those amazing women as they level up and create incredible changes in their lives. They are paving the way for many in the process of leveling up, creating positive changes in their lives, and attracting success in their lives.

The Secret Is To Never Give Up

Creating success and wealth is not an easy journey. It doesn't feel like riding a musical train at Disney World. It can be tough, painful, long, lonely, and very hard at times. The secret is to never give up. The *how* is the million dollar question.

You need to retreat inside of you when it gets too hard to handle, too hard to be. What you retrieve inside of you is resilience, strength, and fortitude. Because what happens at that moment, is that on the vibration scale you are at the lowest, or at the bottom. And to rise up feels immense, overwhelming, and seems impossible.

I have been there, I know what it is. That's the moment when you hold on to that smallest light you can see. It could be just a plant you watch grow every day. Or your child you see becoming more confident with each moment. It can be a song you start loving, or a "never give up" quote you grow to understand more each day. You can also choose to find an expertise for you start mastering a bit more every day.

That progress is you being reborn. And that progress is you emerging like a phoenix from the ashes. Often the deepest pain and the toughest challenges will empower you to grow into your highest self.

This is why I grew through the Believe-Act-Lead Method by seeing how it helped women quantum leap into a higher version of themselves. Just like Yasmine launched her new old jeans recycling brand after a big impact of the pandemic on her Communication Agency. Similarly, Sandra was nominated board member in a large, international financial institution after regaining confidence and honoring herself with respect, love, and appreciation. Daily work and a morning routine proved incredibly efficient. And also Firdaous got a high-level executive position at an international investment bank after two years of health struggle.

By being in the midst of these incredible ladies, I felt how I was helping. Plus, the role I was playing helped me feel useful and valued. It was a way for me to reconnect with my mission more and more and to embody it truly. I also grow and power up every day and I mature in the role I know I'm destined to play. This is possible because I deeply believe in the infinite power of the divine and that everything happens for a reason.

When I was stuck for two years, I couldn't see the wisdom from the bitterness of the moment. However, as I look back today, I realize it was feedback from the universe, because I had a bigger calling. Becoming a voice for women brings a thrill I could not have discovered without going through pain, reaching rock bottom, and pushing myself up again. I know what it is to be hurt, betrayed, and lose everything you've ever worked for.

I created a roadmap to success from my own journey and my own rebirth.

If you are feeling stuck in daily habits and frustrated with the day being too short to get everything you've planned completed, I've put together a recipe that helped me and hundreds of women to date.

As a visionary woman who wants to impact the lives of multiple people with her business, I know what it's like to be juggling so many things at once. I can also relate to the frustration you might feel when things seem chaotic or out of your control.

What we need to understand is that our state, on a daily basis, dictates the type of results we create for ourselves, and in order to be successful, we cannot be operating out of a place of frustration. In order to get into the frequency of reaching success, you need to first trust the process of creation and of business growth. Nothing happens overnight, so keep a success mindset throughout the journey.

Because we all function with energy, you need to clear yourself from all the energy that isn't serving. That will be all the past mistakes, failures, setbacks, or anything that didn't go the way you wanted. You must honor yourself and stand for your word as if it was a law. In practical terms, it means that your most important objective is to seek excellence in your expertise by pushing yourself to become greater tomorrow in what you do than how you are today. In addition, honoring yourself means treating yourself with respect and consideration. This is how you would work on your self-image so that you build a strong belief about your success and that you deserve the best.

Finally, have faith despite the obstacles and the struggles, and believe in your intuition and the power inside of you to guide you to reach the success you are seeking. Make up your mind and carry out the decision to shift your attitude and seek success and excellence because you deserve the best life.

This is an invitation to power together and to empower more women to do the same. The ripple effect will transform generations of women; the world needs to see them shining through their leadership and sustainable impact.

Honor Yourself and Feel the Harmony

It all starts with how you treat yourself. When you make the decision that you're no longer feeling sick of being stuck, honor your word and make it so solid that you have no choice but to respect it.

Honor yourself in everything that you do. Even when you feel that you're not happy with the work you have done. You finish a book, and as soon as you publish it, you don't like it anymore. Or you finish a project, and as soon as you present it, you don't like it anymore.

Each time you finish something that you have created in your mind in the past, you evolve from it. It's normal that you feel that you can do it better. With time, we grow and we improve our way of doing things. But this doesn't stop you from honoring yourself. Honoring yourself is celebrating what you have finished, and getting ready to improve as you grow to a new level.

Don't get yourself into a sabotage mode because you aren't in a position to cheer yourself on about what you have created, because it's not the way you want to see yourself. Don't feel bad about something you did or a work you just finished because it wasn't quite right. Respect your efforts and how you're evolving.

Honor the past version of you, because that version is the one which created who you are today. If you have better ideas today than what you did before, you still need to honor and express gratitude for what you have done.

When you don't honor yourself, it's like saying no to the universe for what you receive. By honoring yourself, you'll be expressing more of the gratitude you need to ground yourself and to set up the foundation for you to attract what you desire.

It's about honoring your past with the good and the bad parts of it, honoring your evolution as it comes to you. That means you embrace the evolution of who you become as it comes with its own speed. If it's faster than you can grasp, let it happen because growth is coming fast. If it is slow, trust that things are being prepared and will show up. At the moment, you need to be able to believe with every fiber of your being that the universe is doing its part to create what you are expecting. At that moment, you need to trust and have faith, even if there is no evidence. When you're able to harmonize with the universe, the divine, and Mother Nature, you can start making the most beautiful results in your life. I love what Napoleon Hill writes in his book, *Think and Grow*

Rich: "when it comes, it comes pouring." You have to trust it. The ultimate music when there's the perfect harmony and all the experiences are displayed one after the other, creating the puzzle of a life of greatness for you. That harmony happens when you start seeing beauty in joy and sadness. It's about finding power in weakness. That harmony sheds light on the significance of what you do and your alignment with your inner life. **Magic happens when you harmonize.**

You don't need to change who you are or where you are to change your life. You don't need to do different things to succeed. You don't need to change everyone around you to turn your life around.

You need to stop feeling wrong about yourself. You need to start accepting yourself and loving yourself as you are.

Incredible changes occur when you allow them to. They can be as tiny as the way you feel inside when you do the same things you do every day. The way you pour yourself a cup of tea or coffee every morning, the way you look at yourself in the mirror before you leave your house to go to a meeting, to run an errand, or to simply go for a walk. You can change your life when you decide to do so. You can change your life when you truly honor yourself and your word.

Stay in alignment, focus on the significance of what you do, trust the process, let the universe harmonize with you, and it will come pouring when it comes.

My Workbook - Chapter 1

What is my roadmap?

What makes a happy life for me?

How does my culture define a woman's role?

How will I stand out?

2

The Roadmap to Success

In the toughest moments, I woke up in the morning hoping that it was a nightmare and that my office was fine and the team was waiting for me to kick start the day and prepare for our big meeting or big conference. Unfortunately, it was real. I had to wake up and hate myself every day for so long before surrendering and understanding how to change.

Within those moments, I still needed to show up as the loving mother. This was so hard. The children had nothing to do with my challenging professional life and deserved a life of joy and happiness. What if I was able to smile again? What if I was able to dance and sing with them?

Coming out from the deepest and darkest hole any entrepreneur worries about took time, consistency, and perseverance.

Where do you start when you wake up in the morning and decide that this is not the life that you want? When you know that you could have made things better? That feeling when you know there's a missing link that you didn't find yet and you don't know what it is. So, you think in your head, *If only I worked a little bit harder, or understood the market a little better, or spent more time marketing or improving my offer, product, business, network, or relationships, things would have been different.*

We all know that feeling in your body, in your stomach. Or that node that you feel when you breathe. In your throat, in your lungs even though you know you should relax, take it easy. You work through it by doing your favorite yoga pose, or your meditation soundtrack. You add to that some relaxing music or an upbeat song to cheer you up!

Still, that node is there. It doesn't want to go away. The feeling comes back. There's only one small step missing to reach the success you deserve.

But you don't see it coming yet. Where is it?

I understand that feeling very much. Three years ago, I felt stuck in an overwhelming professional dilemma. At that moment, I was feeling that a piece was missing in my puzzle of life, but I didn't know what it was.

I learned the hard way that business isn't supposed to always go smoothly. There are times when you can win a lot, and moments where the risks kick in and you can lose as much or more.

There's a dual approach to everything. Positive and negative. Masculine energy and feminine energy. Success and failure. Great wins and potential losses. It applies to everything. When you can be prepared for the potential of losing everything, winning becomes your only pathway.

In simple words, it means that you have to be prepared to handle the challenges, the difficulties, and the setbacks. To thrive and unlock the channel of abundance and attract success in your life, you need to be ready for it. It starts by being able to let go of the strong desire for things and surrender to the symphony of the universe that prepares your journey the way you expect to be. You could have never crafted the how of your life, of your goal, and of your dream better than what the divine and the universe unfolded for you. That's the beauty of how the symphony of your life is playing when you surrender, it will be out of this world.

What Does Success Mean?

Success has different definitions and meanings. It depends on the person, context, ambitions, and the inner values.

On the one hand, success can be evaluated and defined through material achievements, money, assets, or fame. On the other, success is aligned with inner peace, fulfillment, or feeling joy, love, and happiness.

In reality, success is very specific to you. Success is the reflection of your being in a situation where you feel you have fulfilled what "having a good life" means to you. And "having a good life" could be about reaching your inner peace, having good health, and enjoying loving relationships. Thus, success in that sense has nothing to do with material ownership.

If your excitement, motivation, and stimulation are about creating wealth and making an impact, the closer you get to those goals, the more you will feel you are approaching success. Therefore, success will be seen relative to what you have defined as a celebratory achievement. And this celebration point will keep moving when you have a long-term horizon for your vision. This way success will become a journey and not an end on its own.

It Starts With a Broad Perspective

Broadening your perspectives will help you keep the focus and not sabotage yourself. This is particularly important when you feel you aren't achieving small objectives with the tight deadlines you gave yourself.

We set goals to stay focused and know where we are going.

However, you should never let those goals become an emotional triggering factor when you find yourself at your lowest state and the goals appear too far or too difficult. This is why when you define a goal to reach 1k, 10k, 100K, or even 1 million this month, as soon as the month finishes and you don't see that goal becoming a reality, you get yourself into a spiral of frustration and unworthiness.

The same thing happens when you are looking for a new job, a new partner, or anything you are seeking to manifest in your life.

When your goal is big, failure, setbacks, or a month with no results will not stop you from reaching it. Because the picture is larger. The dream is broader. The horizon is long-term. This way, the mission holds many stories in it and your context will make the journey worth it. With its ups and downs. This is how you build resilience.

When you create a strong belief about your mission, you can make it extremely powerful and aligned with who you really are. In addition, when you keep your goals and objectives broad, they become your legacy. This way you won't get into a self-sabotaging mood as soon as something doesn't go your way.

Finally, when you can zoom out from the difficulties and consider the larger picture that means that you are acting from a solid equilibrium you have built for yourself.

Success Is About Balance

The meaning of success changes from one person to another. It depends on the norms, perception, culture, emotional state, ambitions, and the overall context. Despite different meanings, it all comes down to finding the right balance in every aspect of life.

Transcending every facet of life.

Success is therefore about finding the Balance between mindset and strategy, logical reasoning and intuition. It's also striking the equilibrium between finding excuses and growing resilient. Taking an actionable plan and keeping a strategic vision. Being super productive while enjoying peace of mind.

We all look for that balance where we can manage our daily responsibilities and be productive at the same time. That balance is a way to thrive in parallel with your professional life and your personal life. From an energetic perspective, this means balancing the masculine and feminine side of it, and stepping up to spirituality while being grounded in the three-dimensional reality.

This is why I created the BAL Method to empower women by embracing that Balance in every aspect of their life. Because the first step to a better life is to find that balance and what it means to each one of you. This balance is the way you can find yourself driven towards your goals and objectives by a wave that feels harmonious and fulfilling, making it sound like a beautiful symphony in the making.

When you are too much on one side and not on the other, it affects you not only your life, but also your business and all the results you receive in life. Your results are about your income, clients, business, happiness, confidence, family, and your well-being.

Success will then become a natural next step when you stand on five pillars creating a solid equilibrium:

1. spirituality
2. mental and physical health
3. relationships
4. profession
5. money

You can excel in one or two pillars, but something will always feel missing if you don't give it your all. This is why it's important to design your equilibrium. Just as if you were to design your own table and build upon it to greatness. The solidity of the foundations will make it possible to build on top of it, however much your dream takes you to build and create.

Thus, once you reach the balance for these five pillars, you will find a fulfilling equilibrium where success shines all through.

In your daily endeavors, success is about the balance between mindset and strategy, intuition and logical reasoning, finding excuses and growing resilient, and making actionable plans and keeping a strategic vision. This balance will provide the equilibrium between your professional life and personal life. When you find yourself standing on that equilibrium, you will feel driven towards your goals and objectives by a wave that seems magically harmonious and fulfilling.

Balance and Harmony are Like Math and Music

This is the essence of what the BAL Method is about—standing on a strong balance. My primary objective was to help women achieve

Balance in every aspect of life and to stay aligned with the inner values and the overall objectives. Through the three phases, women are able to redesign their thinking and their actions. All in harmony with their personalities and their aspirations. This is why and how they can set a bigger stage for themselves so they let their genius shine for them and become a magnet to all the possibilities. The Believe, Act, and Lead approach is how you can redesign your thinking and actions, all in harmony with your personality and aspirations.

In fact, when you are too much on one side and not on the other, there will be a direct correlation with the results that you get for yourself. Those results will represent the level of income, clients, business, happiness, confidence, family, well-being, and all the other aspects of life.

I learned that balance early on when I was spending hours mastering problem-solving in mathematics and physics, and taking a break from it to enjoy playing piano and practicing to reach excellence. Making music and learning Chopin's Nocturnes, the Goldberg Variations by Bach, or a piece from Mozart or Beethoven, was as valuable to me as all the other schoolwork.

Embracing these two ways of being simultaneously kept me focused as a student, as a graduate, and also in the early years of my career. And as I was advancing, my spark became the mission I deeply believed in: playing a role in sustainable development and making a difference in people's lives.

When you're able to design the appropriate balance for you, you will find a real harmony in your life. That harmony will become your field of awareness and will open up new dimensions for the possibilities and the success that you can attract in your life. **The journey to success is yours to create and that is the beauty of it!**

Finding the balance in life is becoming more and more at the center of debates around self-development and personal well-being while thriving in business and in the professional sphere. For women in particular, finding a balance is not an option.

Thus, being a woman is equivalent to playing several roles at the same time. A woman has to optimize her time and her energy between being a mother, a wife, and a daughter on one hand, and a professional, a leader, and a CEO on the other.

Finding the balance is a way of being and feeling present and respected in the different spaces where you belong. At home, the office, and in your community. This means giving yourself the permission to organize your time in a way that you give every part of your life the attention and the time it deserves.

There are many sacrifices to be made. Many tough moments to go through. Through all of these different moments, balance finds itself as a way of being, a lifestyle. It makes you feel fulfilled and responsible at the same time.

Integrating that new lifestyle can happen with a thorough time management scheme, discipline, and a deep understanding of the five pillars.

Five Pillars to Create a Solid Equilibrium

There are five essential pillars to build on in order to design a balanced life. They need to be growing in parallel and developing all at the same time.

1. Spiritual Aspect

This is your understanding of the infinite intelligence, the cosmos, the universe, and the divine light. The spiritual aspect varies depending on your belief, religion, faith, your understanding of the universe, and of life's creation ... depending on how you feel about that bigger force and the bigger light that holds all of us. When you are able to zoom out of the three-dimensional reality—the one we see, feel, hear, sense—you can feel connected to a power bigger than you, bigger than us. That power is the understanding of a light that holds all up. This is what is described as the zone, a space where everything happens effortlessly. That area between your daily thoughts and the bigger power. It feels like a space without gravity. A space where you can sense and feel supernatural possibilities and a place where you can believe in magic and extraordinary power.

The way you can feel that you reach that level of being and understanding is when you are in peace and contentment with yourself. In fact, when you can connect with your inner power, you can reach real peace of mind and find yourself in a lasting state of relaxation.

At that moment, you will become more in tune with yourself and more creative. You will also start feeling and hearing your intuition. That intuition will become your torch in the darkness, your light when you move towards the success, growth, and evolution you are set up to have.

That state of higher spirituality will help you get in harmony with the laws of the universe, which make things go around. They make a plant grow when you water a seed in the ground, or an apple fall from the tree to the ground because of gravity. Those laws make evolution feel normal when you are synchronized with them and when you understand to trust that cosmic light. What does it mean?

Understanding the universal light and the infinite intelligence took me back to my days of sitting in physics class, learning about quantum physics and duality. In the world of twelve dimensions, things are different. They are beyond our graphic imagination. It's a place where an electron doesn't have an algorithmic pattern, but it follows a pattern out of this world. Understanding that world makes you understand how you can quantum leap to another space of possibilities.

When you apply that to your life, you surrender to the universal power and you create true harmony with the universe. At that moment, you become lighter than the heaviness of problems and burdens. You also free yourself from the invisible glass ceiling, the box where you found yourself stuck with all beliefs, culture, and a voice in your head corrupted by discouraging news and numbers about women reaching leadership positions and creating seven and eight figure companies.

Believing truly and profoundly in the power of a bigger force and being connected with the infinite light.

Even from a scientific perspective, as an engineer I always come back to the science and how it works. Therefore, by deepening your understanding of science, you will find yourself getting closer to spirituality. When scientists went deeper studying atoms, electrons, and photons, they reached the quantum field. And the only way scientists explain the quantum field, they use the word light. There are no objects in the quantum field, only energetic waves of light. That's when you start understanding the existence of sixth sense and that ultrasound dimension you can't see, hear, or smell, but you can intuitively feel it around you. Just like there is an invisible force or team around you. Depending on how you command and trust that team, it will or will not assist you to reach your ultimate objective.

The spiritual dimension is what makes a difference in everything you do. Once you grasp it as its meaning unfolds through this book, you will realize that even doing business is spiritual.

As a consequence, you will achieve your goals and reach incredible success. This very aspect will strengthen your faith and help you go through your journey to success, wealth, and time freedom.

Finding meaning in the simplest event can become a source of magic in your life. Glorifying and celebrating events such as the new year, the full moon, the start of the lunar month, have an energetic overflow. It makes it easier to believe in miracles and to start manifesting incredible wealth, love, health, and relationships. Everything you want exists in the energetic world, but being able to feel it and sense it will bring it closer to you. Each one of us has different portals to access that non-physical, spiritual and energetic realm. The more you do so, the more you can hold in your hand what you desire most. That's what I call manifestation.

We usually focus on what we know and we expect what we know. When we free ourselves from those references, we start opening to more possibilities. That's where the paradigm shift becomes essential if you want to quantum leap to a new dimension of money, love, joy, luxury, and whatever reference you have in your success metrics.

Leveling up from a spiritual perspective will make manifestation not attached to yourself and to your ego anymore, but to what you know and your brain accepts as logic. Manifestation will be seen as an opportunity with no stress attached to it. An opportunity and a whole new experience of life. You will then use it to plant a seed in the quantum field and to say that today it has meaning and use that energy to feel that you are connected with the bigger force of the cosmos. It is possible to manifest in that frequency.

2. Health Aspect

Take a moment to evaluate how much time you are spending in the health department. This includes eating habits, exercising, and having a healthy lifestyle. When I was a child, I had a quote from the middle ages that was repeated to us in Arabic over and over in textbooks and was stuck in my mind. "A sound mind in a sound body." It has so much wisdom that wise philosophers and scientists were abound by.

Having a healthy lifestyle will give you the energy you need to become successful in business and to feel continuous motivation. And having a lifestyle means that you are honoring yourself, your body, and the amazing person you are.

Whatever stage you are at in your life, there are some fundamentals that you cannot ignore. The top of these fundamentals is your health. You need to be on top of your health, which means exercising and eating healthy. If you don't have the stamina and you feel exhausted all the time, you will never be able to bring any passion to your relationships nor to your business.

You can define the best plan, find the best gym, find the best trainer, and start the workout. However, this isn't what will make you change or get fit. All you need is to tell yourself to "get moving." You can do that on your own, ten minutes a day, and your body will start reacting to that and feeling how you are bringing some positive actions to you.

It's not hard to figure out how to get fast results when you decide that you are changing your lifestyle around and taking over your health.

It is obvious that when you feel fit, you make different decisions, you take different actions. And it always comes down to the healthy energy inside of you. It gives you stamina, power, and makes you want to take on your day, the challenges, and everything that comes with it.

What you are going to believe about health and energy will transform what you believe about everything around you. That belief is of course not enough. You need to create a sustainable experience so that you can not only have a solid base, but you can ensure that it lasts. Change won't happen overnight. You can go to the gym, come back, and check your figure in the mirror, but nothing will be different. You can go again tomorrow, and will still not see any changes. It's the consistency and the persistence that will bring you a fit body. Just like eating healthy.

This is why you need to challenge yourself so that you grow in the process. Give yourself the challenge of running a mile or a kilometer, or doing yoga every day. You can do the same thing with the food you eat, the sleep you get, or how you treat yourself. With every new progress, celebrate yourself because that will strengthen your foundation and make you improve even more.

What do you get from having focus in your life? It's really improving the energy in your body. So, your energy becomes the vibrant way of being and the natural state we are in. Because energy is life. The more you have the energy, the more you will feel better in everything you do, every project you take, every new relationship you enter into.

You think better when your body is fit and healthy. Walking or integrating ten minutes of exercise into your daily routine will improve your physiology and change it to help you thrive and keep motivated.

Integrate a schedule where you can get yourself fit, eat healthily, and have a healthy lifestyle. Eating well means having a balanced regime with fruits and vegetables, protein and lipids, and all you need to keep your energy high and get all the toxins out of your body. There are so many programs to get rid of all the toxicity in the body. Programs in connection with fasting, or drinking celery, lemon juice, or any other ingredient with cleansing characteristics.

Mental health is just as important by reducing stress, toxicity, and pressure on your mental well-being. This isn't a luxury or something you leave for later. This is the way you save yourself from burnout and depression, and most importantly from psychosomatic diseases.

Making mental and physical health a central aspect of your life is very important. If you reach millions or even a billion dollars, you can only enjoy it when your health is at the top.

3. Personal and Relational Aspect

This aspect is related to how *you* see yourself and how you nurture the relationships around you. This pillar is about understanding the power of love—love for yourself and others.

As social animals, we feel good and happy when we are connected, when we love and we feel loved.

It all starts by truly loving yourself. By being proud of who you are and who you have come to be, after the years of working hard, of trying, of failing and standing back up, or being in the process of making sense to all that you are going through.

You will understand that when you can assess how you feel about who you truly are when no one is watching. How are you treating yourself? Do you feel respect? Do you feel shame? Do you feel pride? Or do you feel worthlessness?

Question yourself. Take an empty page and write all the thoughts that come to your mind about you, about how you feel about you.

You will be surprised. The one percent that make it to the top of the wealth and the success in the world manage somehow to become their own cheerleader. If you don't have that cheering voice overarching all the others, you need to do something about it today. At this moment, put a seed in your mind for what you want the best of you to tell yourself, and make it your mantra. A continuous mantra such as:

- I am happy and grateful that I attract respect and appreciation.
- I am happy and grateful that wherever I go, I win and prosper.
- I am happy and grateful that money comes to me from different sources and on a continuous basis.

Things don't change just because you say so or think you can. Deep change happens when you redesign your paradigm, when you are able to find the voice deep in you and install it through daily discipline, perseverance, and building a strong habit of being.

Alone is not enough. Alone is not even possible.

There are new trends to go and sit for two weeks or forty days far away in a secluded area to ponder on yourself. It will calm you down, it can be the start of a spiritual path. But this is not what gives you the courage to thrive, create, grow, or attract wealth and infinite possibilities. Finding the courage comes from outside of you. It's the love, caring, and affection from the relationships you have created around you that makes it happen.

Creating fulfilling relationships is essential for you to thrive and attract incredible abundance in your life.

It all starts with discipline to nurture your most important relationships, to bring love and compassion to all of them, discovering and integrating into your life the taste of unconditional love. In any relationship, there is some misunderstanding and miscommunication, but you know deep inside that the soul is connected and that the survival instinct of the animal in each one of us can make things seem different or hurtful to the other person in a relationship.

So always put the other person you love first, because in a relationship it isn't about you or your ego. When you have a problem in a relationship, you feel pain because you are focused on yourself and not your partner. Shift the focus to the other person and trust that their intentions are pure deep inside. By truly believing and knowing that there is no negative intent, you shift your attitude. It makes apologizing easier and deeper.

Again, it takes discipline to have the courage to share the vulnerability. **The more vulnerable you are, the more power you will have.** This means learning to love no matter what. You'll be able to do that when you love yourself unconditionally and you start to see beyond the survival instinct of your partner, your friends, and whoever you care for. There is a distinction between human behavior and the human spirit.

While human spirit has perfection in it, human behavior is always a reflection of the animal inside of us. So forgive yourself for relationships that didn't work the way you wanted or any hurtful words you said to someone.

If you want to have an extraordinary relationship, you need to nurture that relationship with discipline so that you can integrate new habits that help you put the feelings and love of the other person before your ego.

Thus, absolute courage and vulnerability, learning to love no matter what, starts by loving yourself no matter what. This means you tell the truth, because you know that everything is okay and being genuine and vulnerable is more rewarding and powerful than being obsessed by the idea that you are going to feel the pain.

Discipline is important because it helps you instill the habit. Otherwise, the regrets from not having tried, or not having done enough, will be very heavy on your shoulders.

Finally, there is the true power of love, adoration, and praise. It raises your vibration and those around you, which will keep it at a high level and help you attract all the wellness and the wealth you are seeking in your life. This is how we understand that the only reason why we get into a relationship is to magnify our human emotions. A simple example is when you are happy and excited and something good happens in your life, you want to share it with someone who is going to feel that joy with you.

The way you can nurture those relationships that are important for you and your emotional well-being is by discipline and by being truly present. Presence—giving the space of listening and truly caring—is what draws people to each other.

It's true that women's brains, with their diffused awareness, experience multiple conversations at one time, while men focus on one thing at a time.

If you are a man in a relationship and you are in your head and the woman is looking to connect with you, if she doesn't feel that presence, it's because you are too much in your head. You need to be connected emotionally and have a clear and positive vision about where the relationship is going. Nothing will thrive if there is no vision of where it is going.

Finally, these are important questions to help you work on your self-image and your self-esteem. Everything great you want to create starts with the way you see yourself and value it.

The personal aspect also includes your relationship within your family and your friendships. It's been said and repeated that your life is the average of the five people surrounding you. Thus, it is essential to surround yourself with like-minded people and friends who are encouraging you to reach success and to create a life that you are working towards.

4. Professional Aspect

This aspect is related to your work and your profession. It is at the center for professionals as it represents the drive of their careers and their financial well-being. Nevertheless, it is essential to become an expert in a field that you love and feel connected with. Because when you are aligned with what you love and what you do, you can create an amazing impact, all while feeling fulfilled. And to become an expert in the field of your choice, one of the common assessments is you must spend ten thousand hours studying and mastering that very field.

How did you find yourself in the professional life you have created for yourself, or you have attracted to your life?

The story behind it is very important to be on top of it and to embody your profession in alignment with who you are. Because you want to feel happy about your professional life and about the journey, it is helping you.

I started as an engineer in my academic career because I wanted to be like my father and follow in his steps. I had put this seed in my mind from such an early age that it became a natural move. I even had these thoughts about how I was ready to be the only girl in the class. Because in the eighties very few women went to engineering schools, let alone had a successful engineering career. We didn't have a lot of role models around us. My father became mine and got me ready to pave the way for other young girls and young women to do the same.

In the choice of my career and the next job I was seeking and applying to, I always looked for alignment with the role I wanted to play. My interest in being an engineer was tightly linked to my drive to understanding how to transfer technology so that I can contribute to the development of my country and my region of the world.

So my internship was about spending time in large, international corporations and understanding how they do work in different parts of the world. I spent time in Schlumberger, in a Thermal Power Production site, as an engineer to understand the way real work was being done and how we could actually apply what we learned at school. As I deepened my understanding of economic development and environmental sustainability, I wanted to be part of the large institutions as they contributed to creating a world free of poverty and played a central role in development and capacity building. I loved every part of my professional journey at the World Bank working in different countries on development-related sectoral strategies in Latin America, South East Asia, and the Middle East and North African region.

After this I came back to Morocco where I joined the Prime Minister as an economic advisor, continuing my work with extreme passion for development and setting up strategies.

Everything after that followed my interest in strategy, development, and finance. The drive to get that love for your job and for the work you're doing and creating about you is about keeping the "why" behind everything you do.

What is your *why*?

Take time as you read through this book to pause and remember the *why* behind everything you do and everything you think about. Why are you getting up every day?

Why are you continuously trying to be better? Why are you looking for ways to stand out? Why are you seeking excellence? And why, deep inside, do you want to believe so much in yourself and in your work?

Looking for your true *why* helps you find the calling and drive in you. This is how you can find that spark in you. When you answer these questions and are able to pinpoint your *why*, let it grow and guide you to reach the level of success you thrive for.

I did this over and over each time I was faced with challenges in my professional life and needed to recreate myself. I had to remember the *why* behind my working hard. The *why* behind the long nights I spent studying mathematics and physics, when I woke up in the middle of the night to go over my lessons and the exercises.

I held on to that *why* during the long nights I spent at Harvard University finalizing a model or a research paper. I still remember vividly, that night when we worked so late and we needed to print the report in several copies and bind it nicely before presenting in the morning. It was snowing and so cold as we crossed Harvard Yard to go to Kinkos. The printing shop was open twenty-four hours; there was no internet at that time in the mid-nineties, and we had to do everything on our own. We were so cold, exhausted but excited about a job well finished. We knew —myself and two other students—that our professor, Peter Rogers, would be happy and astonished in the morning. We loved to surprise him and to show him that we were capable of so much and that he made the best choice to take us as his PhD students.

Working hard with a noble cause and a beautiful fulfillment—a drive that makes life delicious and exciting.

Later, that habit of working hard and being on top of my work became just a normal way of being. I enjoyed every piece of it, because I kept my true why and how my professional life was aligned with what I really wanted.

It wasn't only acceptable but most enjoyable to spend long days and weekends at the World Bank preparing high-level meetings and undertaking faraway missions. The long meetings, the long hours of writing, presenting, analyzing, understanding, and coordinating were done from a space of gratitude for learning, contributing, and having a meaningful job.

So, what kept me going when I felt overwhelmed was knowing my true mission. What kept me going when I was stuck during my entrepreneurship journey and when it felt too hard was remembering my true purpose. This purpose was my deep belief in my mission and the role I have been prepared to play for many years in sustainable development and making a difference in people's lives.

Your purpose and your mission are not your daily job. It's that bigger context that broadens your horizon and opens up your consciousness.

It's important to know your mission and your purpose so that you can connect to jobs that feel aligned with what makes you feel alive and happy. You can change it depending on the season of your life, or the circumstances around you.

This happened to me, during the most challenging time of my corporate career. I felt the need for a reset. A need to recreate me differently. Thus, two years ago, I channeled a clear and vivid role of becoming a catalyst for women's empowerment and leadership.

This is *why* my mission today is to restore gender equality around leadership, wealth creation, and making a sustainable impact. My mission is to help women grow confident, resilient, tech-savvy, and financially free. This way, they will uplevel wealth creation to a new level and the ripple effect will make it possible to improve the life of a billion young girls and young women.

Today, I believe so strongly that gender equality is at the root of every facet of sustainability. This is how we can prepare for a sustainable future!

Find your *why* and make it so big that it overwhelms you and drives you far, and create your professional journey around it.

5. Money Aspect

Are your finances the way you want them to be? Are you happy with the amount of money you are making at the end of the month and the end of the year?

These questions are related to your capacity to attract money into your life and your paradigm when it comes to money.

We grow up believing that it's difficult to attract money and that we need to work very hard to get money. This money paradigm can block you from attracting abundance and from feeling that you deserve to be wealthy. This is why shifting this money blockage is the only way to step away from the energy of scarcity and get ready to receive abundance and improve your money situation.

This pillar is about your relationship with money and about your paradigm. This pillar is how you can get yourself into the money vortex. Using the energetics language, it's about accessing the money channel.

There's an abundance of money around you. When you understand how to frame this relationship and how to connect with the energy of money, you can tap into the abundance of money, whether you want to be in the service business, you are launching a new project, or you want to attract investment.

You can always improve the level of money in your life by making the decision to do so and discipline yourself to recreate the wealth and attract it in your life.

The further I deepen my work on mindset and energetics, the more I understand that there's a force bigger than ourselves and an energy around the flow of money. But in a simple way, you can do something about the financial part of your life. If what you are making at the end of the month doesn't give the autonomy you are looking for, get the skills to improve your wealth and to be able to provide a higher level of service and be paid for it.

When we focus so much on the difficulty of making money, the bills, or the debts, that becomes everything we have in our mind. And we know for sure that where the focus goes energy goes. So choose what to focus on from a positive perspective instead and make all your energy go for it. In parallel, set up a clear strategy and a plan to improve your financial situation.

People became millionaires starting from absolutely nothing. Unicorns are born every day: these are the billion-dollar companies. It takes discipline, perseverance, a strong will, and focus to reach incredible levels and surprise everyone around. You can be the next one in your family who breaks the pattern of wealth creation if you choose to. When you feel that you don't know how, get help. You can access so much valuable information for free on the internet and by reading books. There are also mentors and coaches who have done it before, changing their life around and helping thousands and thousands of people do the same in different industries.

I strongly believe that everyone deserves to have a financially autonomous life and create the wealth he or she wishes to have. There's so much abundance out there, that there is more than enough for each one to attract and create the levels they look for. It takes believing in it, acting on it by articulating a focused strategy, and translating it into concrete action plans. Above all, it's about trusting the process and having faith that things will work out for the best. Money is yours to take, claim it!

Success and Fulfillment

Reaching success and creating wealth are the tangible results everyone is looking forward to. They can be the driving force when they come within a balanced life. Or they can become a daily struggle and the whole balance is weakened.

This is why, when you understand that keeping the balance among those five aspects is the most important task to focus on, you can define your map to greatness on a solid foundation. Starting with the spiritual and health aspects, both physical and mental, you get ready to tackle all the other aspects. And notice that the professional aspect which is often considered wrongly the first comes after the relationship aspect.

This is why the B-A-L Method starts with a thorough and deep mindset shift. When you work on your mindset, everything else comes easily. In fact, with the right mindset, you expand the possibility to have, receive, and get more of what you desire.

This is why the first step of Believe also sets the ground for finding that balance in your life and understanding how the five pillars can make you thrive and go beyond your possibilities. Mindset is what makes people join the one percent of the population who owns ninety-six percent of the wealth in the world.

I have so much incredible passion and love for the process that I have created to help myself, women, and also men, to change their lives and reach new levels of possibilities. And this is what you can sense throughout the pages of the book.

It all starts with you switching to an abundance mindset. You are ready to embrace opportunities and to see them when they come around. Sometimes people hide behind their faith so that they can avoid making tough decisions.

Decisions are considered tough when they contradict your comfort zone, your way of getting by in life, and when they entail taking risks.

To thrive, reach success, and create wealth, it's essential to work on all these aspects simultaneously. Feeling fulfilled means that the five pillars are all integrated into your journey to a successful and balanced life.

The second phase of the process is taking action and doing the work. It takes discipline, strategy, and thorough planning to be able to launch a professional project, set up multiple sources of income, and simply improve your well-being.

Combining action with faith and trusting the system will allow you to reach not only new levels but create streams of abundance. It takes perseverance, dedication, and discipline.

Finally, the third phase is about harnessing your leadership skills and understanding what it means to make an impact. Everyone has a role to play in creating a better future for the world and ensuring sustainable development.

By understanding how to make an impact and give incredible value, it makes you approach doing business in a different way. It comes down to serving and helping others. Thus, by focusing on creating so much value, and bringing excellence in everything you do, money will flow in and appreciation will come your way.

My Workbook - Chapter 2

What does success look like for me?

What are my personal goals and objectives?

What are my professional goals and objectives?

What is my why?

3

Overcoming Struggles and Challenges

Day by day, I started appreciating my garden. The hortensia the gardener planted in different parts of the house began to blossom. I chose blue and purple for the back door, and pink in the front door. Every day, I watched them blossom. The blue and purple were all pink, and the pinks turned different shades of pink. I was smiling the moment I woke up and stepped out the door to see them. Each day, it made me feel a little bit more happy. I talked about hortensia to my children and my husband all day long. They were filling me with joy, and that joy came from knowing that nature was abundant and continuously available to everyone. The beauty of nature was out there for you to grab. Meditation started to make more sense because I brought everything back to my hortensias. As if I had witnessed the creation of something extraordinary from the dark soil. Beautiful colors, beautiful shapes. Plus, the intrigue of what I would discover in the morning was getting more and more thrilling. Gratitude came naturally; the flowers were part of my list every morning.

There is a healing power in nature and in feeling the abundance of it. There's such a strong energy in nature, because scientifically the atoms in nature have a very high vibration. So you feel peace, love, and calm when you go hiking or when you walk on the beach. That appreciation of infinite beauty triggers something deep in your soul. I train my children to notice nature wherever they are—the leaves in the trees, the never-ending grass, the water in the ocean, the algae, the little, flat rocks by the water, the falling rain. So many of them.

How to Overcome a Struggle?

Having gone through a lot of struggle as an entrepreneur, when I had to close down one of the companies, which turned into having to close the whole holding of companies, I couldn't find the wisdom in it in the beginning. But I knew, deep inside, that there was a reason behind all that I had to go through. Looking back, I realize I was always worried that things might not go right with the funds, the investors, the team, or the portfolio of projects. I was worried about losing everything and feeling stuck. These worries were controlling me and triggering so much anxiety and fear.

It took so much leveling up, wisdom, and healing before realizing that this experience was part of my journey to becoming the person I am today and to not let these thoughts control me anymore. I lived through them all and I survived them stronger, more powered up, and with so much love inside of me, I didn't know I was capable of.

Life has ups and downs. Misfortune can sneak its way in when you least expect it. It can manifest itself through financial and relational stress, a loss, health issues, and injustice. These can drag you down and take over your life when you let them.

Remember, every setback is an opportunity to reclimb back to better success. Successful people have all gone through many challenges and struggles. What they had in common is that they never gave up. They kept on trying, falling, and standing back up.

In one of his famous speeches, Winston Churchill told his audience to, "never give in." Churchill has been quoted saying that, "success is the ability to move from one failure to another without loss of enthusiasm."

In business and in your life, if you want to reach success and high-level results, you need to take risks, and taking risks will come with their own setbacks and struggles.

At times, the suffering and the pain from a setup can be overwhelming. It can be so big that you won't be able to find any reason for you to keep going. That is the moment where you need to make a choice for your life. Will you be carrying a backpack full of heavy rocks from your past? Or will you lighten up and start fresh?

By Building Resilience

Being able to overcome a struggle or a difficulty comes down to your resilience.

Resilience is your ability to restart fresh every day. It allows you to take an empty page every morning and rewrite your journey, without carrying bitterness, pain, or suffering from past experiences.

When you understand resilience profoundly, you understand that it is the start of your connection with spirituality. Being able to lean away from a problem or a struggle takes a strong will to do it.

Another way of looking at it is to zoom out and look at the situation you're going through from above.

That zoom out is the beginning of a spiritual leveling up. It helps you stand up from it, allows you to broaden your consciousness and put things in perspective. At that moment, you start understanding the power in you and how to trigger it. This way, you will feel stronger and ready to overcome the hardship of life experiences.

Understanding the Different Forms of Resilience

At the inception of the Bretton Woods financial institutions following the Second World War, the World Bank and the International Monetary Fund saw their role defined as leading institutions to restore postwar countries. They paved the way for the missions of several other international development institutions launched after them. In fact, these institutions have seen their mission change from infrastructure development to the fight against poverty and now to the realization of the 2030 United Nations Sustainable Development Goals (SDG) and all the financial support that comes with it. Nevertheless, the driving force of their mission has always been to strengthen population resilience against environmental and infrastructure degradation, economic, financial, and political challenges. Resilience helps world populations stave off persisting poverty, economic precariousness, and lack of infrastructure. It also makes them embrace capacity building towards local inclusive and sustainable development.

Initially, the concept of resilience was borrowed from physics. The scientific meaning of resilience is indeed connected to materials and bodies' strength against the surrounding shocks and their capacity to restore their shape and their initial characteristics. This notion was integrated into psychological theory describing the capacity of a person to overcome the most complicated events in their lives. In any given community, resilience represents the capacity to restore their sense of living following challenging experiences. In addition, resilience could be applied to a whole region, a group of individuals, or simply to an isolated person. The very ability to stand back up after failure is referred to as "resilience" by the specialists.

People react differently by displaying various stages of resilience. Despite a complicated life and difficult events, some people find a way to restore their happiness and get a normal life after a failure or a terrible event. Other people do the opposite, fall into depression and melancholy. Thus, the capacity to bounce back and to stand back up after falling is equivalent to their degree of resilience. Some need professional help from psychologists and psychoanalysts; others need family and friends' moral support. Their resilience will shape their mental strength and their capacity to cope with problems within their social group and in their work environment.

In the business world, there are not only different ways of being resilient, but also different mechanisms to grow resilient. Often, in the complicated and cruel business environment, where we navigate, resilience seems to be essential and stands in the priority line, along with technical credentials and management skills. To reach success in any discipline, there are several hurdles to overcome. Besides the self-doubt, they include the exams, competitions, interviews, and preparations, in addition to episodes of failures that need to be accepted—it can be a long road. Thus, the type of resilience can dictate the level of success and responsibility any person could reach. Therefore, it is fundamental to reinforce it when it is lacking. The good news is that there are several tools available to help strengthen a person's resilience despite her background or her history, allowing her to overcome the hurdles and come out of the problems stronger and grown up.

Five Steps to Unleash Inner Resilience

Having gone through several business challenges myself, I learned from experience how five simple steps could strengthen oneself and unleash our inner resilience. By following these five simple steps, it becomes then possible not only to reinforce oneself, but to feel completely reborn. Thus, the five main steps to resilience can become a roadmap for each one of us:

1. an internal anger against the struggle and the misfortune
2. a self-inflicted challenge for self-empowerment and inner strength
3. a desire to show strength and endurance to family and friends
4. a sense of humor instead of feeling sorry
5. finding an activity to channel all those emotions through art, spirituality, sports, or any other interest

It's not only important to master these five steps, but to be able to follow them diligently in order to keep your sanity, build self-confidence, and replenish your motivation and enthusiasm. This is the moment where you realize that failure is actually helping you grow stronger and more focused. On the other hand, falling into the victim role will only stave off the reality and deepen the sorrow.

For a woman entrepreneur, this is the time when you envelop yourself with that crocodile skin and navigate through a male-dominated business world while nurturing your own resilience in order to have it ready whenever necessary. Therefore, the best lesson for future generations is to be mentally prepared for life's most challenging events, in order to resist the many destroying shocks on the way.

Life surprises us when we least expect it. Except in the movies, no one would have ever thought that the world could stop for a whole year due to an unknown virus. The scientific and digital developments have bluffed us into believing the invincibility of humanity and nations. The pandemic proved them wrong. The world economy was paralyzed. Human relationships were redefined. Borders were closed in order to contain the virus contagion and to set up the necessary infrastructure for COVID-19 patients. This was the unexpected occasion to check the resilience of our countrywide health infrastructures and security. Fortunately, the vaccine being produced in a record time was most comforting about humanity's giant advances in the science of life and genetics.

In conclusion, at different stages in the business cycle and in our personal lives, resilience is at the center of perseverance, success, development, happiness, and simply life.

With Discipline and Understanding

There are several tools you can use to be able to overcome the hardest moments when you feel in the deepest point of a well or in a dark hole. Studies, research, and life experience are aligned around discipline and a repetitive routine. To accelerate the process, it takes discipline and a mindset shift.

This is how my client, Farah, overcame depression and lack of self-worth after a two-year health struggle. Following the BAL Method[1] program, she strengthened herself up with discipline and understanding, worked on her self-image, and landed the best executive job in London's top Investment Bank.

Similarly, Sofia, who lost her job during the pandemic, didn't have the belief system to launch her own business and rewrite her professional story. Sofia was able to not only start a new recruitment company, she signed her first contract when she started accepting herself the way she is.

The BAL Method program is based on three well-structured phases. First, helping women to start believing in themselves and the possibilities. This first phase is important in all those cases. Understanding how the mind functions makes you go through a whole different direction from depression. The interaction between the conscious mind and the unconscious mind is not taught to us at school nor at the university. If we are lucky, we get our understanding through experiences when we survive them.

Second, act on it by setting a strategic plan. Third, grow as a leader with their inner gifts and talents. Because the BAL Method integrates discipline and mindset shift with a deep understanding of your inner strength and how to use strategic thinking, you are set for life with all the knowledge you need to become in charge of your thoughts.

Any type of freedom comes from discipline and repetition. In fact, both money freedom and time freedom are tightly linked with discipline. And the most important freedom of all is the freedom from your own thoughts and old beliefs.

Once you free yourself from the chains of the past, you become unstoppable.

Understanding Your *Why* Is Power in Itself

I have spent two full years researching how to overcome the most painful difficulties we go through in the different stages of our lives. My research was driven by the desire to find the best strategy to bring myself back to my motivational state and to how I used to master the road map to success and accomplishments within the frame of my old paradigm.

So, my research and understanding were getting deeper than just triggering the rebirth of the phoenix ... it was about restarting with a different paradigm.

Looking at your past, you grow up within a frame limited and structured by your genes, family environment, education, and connections.

And everything you do after that is shaped by those very conditions. To break free from those systematic patterns which are coming from that past, you need to not only understand what the limiting beliefs are that have been inflicted upon you, but also create new habits and integrate a fresh voice more aligned with who you want to become and the goals you want to create, making them yours.

We are tested throughout the years at different levels. It could be from a personal perspective, when relationships become toxic, controlling, or unhealthy. Or from women or men going through a complicated divorce. It could also be from unresolved issues with the parents, siblings, or the family in general.

Difficulties can be encountered at the health level with the manifestation of diseases and problems showing that something needs to be changed.

The mind is connected to every cell of the body. When you are emotionally content and within a state of happiness, every cell of your body feels the same. Oxygen flows in and out with ease and contentment. Your outlook raises up to positivity and your energy will reach high vibration levels.

And of course, in the busy and competitive business environment, a lot of setbacks are related to work, business, and professional life. Struggles and challenges are daily matters. They are part of what business is and what business brings.

Failure is part of the business journey. If you don't encounter a failure, that means you aren't doing anything. You are not trying something new and you are not pushing yourself out of your comfort zone.

It takes courage to rise up to new levels in business, scale up, and seek leadership positions and challenging responsibilities. It also takes the ability to feel the confidence to rise, the confidence to reach new levels of highs. Besides confidence, it requires a strong belief in your bigger context and broader objective.

Any normal life will always have a setback. There are moments when we have happy circumstances and moments when we live in sad and unhappy circumstances. It could be on a fifty-fifty split in terms of percentage, it could be more or less. Either way, we need all of that to feel alive and to push ourselves to grow and to reach new heights

Let's walk through the six phases of grief. Because everyone deserves to come out of that low stage. They deserve to feel the bitterness of difficulties just to remind them that there is something more beautiful and powerful awaiting them.

Mastering the Six Phases of Grief

Strengthening yourself allows you to go through the different phases of grief with ease and good faith.

These six phases are:

Phase 1: Shock and denial are the first reactions to a painful, hurtful experience. You start feeling confused. Fear settles in and you lose confidence and self-esteem. This phase can be dominated by shame and unworthiness when you let the guilt overwhelm you.

Phase 2: Anger from the misfortune brings frustration, irritation, and more anxiety. This could be the manifestation of depression if you stay long in this phase.

Phase 3: Sorrow and sadness follow. These emotions are expected and should just be felt and recognized. You must be able to let go of them.

Phase 4: Finding meaning in the present moment by connecting with others and sharing your story. The objective of this phase is to understand what happens and collect other perspectives.

Phase 5: Acceptance shows up when you are able to look back and say, "It is what it is." At this moment, you break free because you accept the misfortune and you start moving on.

Phase 6: Create a new objective in your life. This phase is the most important one because it signals the start of something new in your life with a more mature goal and a fulfilling mission. Going through the phases of grief makes you grow and harvest a wisdom and an inner power you probably didn't know you had before.

After mastering these six stages, you will feel ready and almost welcoming to those difficult moments. On one hand, it makes you realize that you're stronger than what you thought. On the other, it pushes you to come out of your comfort zone, and that's when you can kickstart a journey of growth and evolution!

Shock and Denial

The first thing that happens when you are faced with a big challenge or something difficult in your life.

Something you're not able to manage, absorb, accept, or even comprehend. It's so unexpected that it is shocking. You're not even sure anymore if it is real or if you are sleeping and having a nightmare. You hope to wake up and see things back to the normal you used to know.

But then you wake, if you're able to sleep at all, and realize that this is the bitter reality. Having gone through a difficult challenge in my professional life as an entrepreneur, I know how it feels to be under the shock of the succession of events. It starts as a big shock for your mind. I found myself taken by a vortex of betrayal, attacks, losses, and everything that goes into the list of entrepreneur's nightmares. The very reason why we don't take the risk to go on and become an entrepreneur, why we prefer to stay in the nine-to-five job so that no risk is taken and there is no getting close to the hint of feeling, experiencing, and being in the middle of entrepreneurial turmoil or corporate complications.

I did have moments where I felt that my whole world was scattered. The "what if" I stayed where I stayed, "what if" I was content with doing the same thing year after year? Moments where I felt that I could have been safer to just be a housewife or stay-at-home mum. Life could have been easier.

However, there was really no time for these questions because I didn't even know I could embody those very roles.

Let's go back to that feeling of denial. You don't think it's possible or true, but events are there to tell you otherwise. So thoughts in your head are spinning. You find yourself painting a darker image and more complications, attracting them to you. Spinning around negativity and seeing more of it every day.

Oh how difficult! Nothing seems to stop it. Nothing.

If I'm sharing this and detailing this cycle of grief it's because I have experienced it hands-on and I discovered the key to open each phase and to feel reborn again. All of this against the odds, and despite what would seem impossible.

I came to self-development and transformation because I needed one. And as I deepened my understanding and my ability to rise back up after having been crushed by the weight of responsibilities and difficulties, I wanted every woman in the world to do so. I wanted every woman in the world to not be afraid of trying and for persevering in her journey to reach success, create wealth, and make an impact.

So this became my calling from the moment I started feeling happy. I began loving myself after having gone through moments where I called myself hateful names, having wrongly felt that I brought this to myself and that everyone was pointing at me.

I have come a long way. Even writing about it wasn't possible for me because I was carrying too much rage and grudges with me.

The day I started seeing innocence in all that happened to me and in the people whom I felt did me wrong at that moment, something deep inside of me shifted forever. That shift is not physical, is not logical, it is spiritual. This is the journey I am taking you through in this book.

In this first phase of shock and denial, and deep hurt, you find yourself emotional in the lowest vibration ever. If we were to analyze the phases as they show up on the Hertz scale of vibration, this will be the lowest ever in terms of level of Hertz.

It's a phase where the shock and denial are equating the similar vibrational level of being ashamed of yourself, or what you are going through. At that level, you will be radiating so much negativity it pulls in a vortex of negative news and events.

Anger

Anger from the misfortune brings frustration, irritation, and more anxiety. This could be the manifestation of depression if you stay long in this phase.

The difficult circumstances translate into anger and rage. Anger against life, against everything that could be blamed on you. The anger is of course for the person who has hurt you or hasn't done things properly to save you from being hurt and experiencing the misfortune.

That anger escalates when you feed it, and feeding it means simply thinking about it continuously by using others to blame, and looking for excuses why life isn't going the way you want it to be.

Anger is one of the most negative emotions and keeps you in a very low vibration. The more you feed the anger, the more it grows. The only one affected by this negativity is yourself when you hold on to it for too long.

This phase is hard to overcome because you get lost in the thinking and drawn by the misfortune. It feels like there is no way out and that the road has been blocked. However, there is no such a thing as the road being blocked. It's your imagination and mental state. Because physically nothing and no one is blocking anything.

Sorrow and Sadness

While feeling sorry for yourself and dwelling in the hurt and the suffering, you're no longer comfortable with people seeing who you are. Because the feeling when I experienced that phase was that I wasn't sure if I was able to say the right thing or if I had to justify myself. You don't want to get into a conversation because you don't want to make a fool of yourself.

These are the times where you will deepen your negative cycle to a depressive state. This enters into the field of Psychiatrists and Psychotherapists. Medical sciences have mastered what needs to be done to rebalance the chemicals in the brain when depression is related to a lack of the production of happy chemicals. In which case, medical supervision becomes necessary.

Feelings are still the same. The hurt is getting amplified and the shock is eating you up if you stimulate yourself in the negative direction each time you think and talk about the problem or the misfortune.

A few clients came to my Empowered Leaders Mastermind at this stage of their grief. They both needed psychiatric help and were given prescriptions. However, having gone through my own transformation and having compared the effect of being grounded through the power of your mind and your spiritual connection, and that of taking Xanax or something similar to be able to go through tough meetings or encounters, I was astonished by the power of the mind. Because it has the same effect but it keeps your capacity to feel happy. While drugs numb you completely, they may actually add to your depression because you are no longer able to feel any satisfaction from anything happy. You become numb all around.

Laura is from France. She was feeling depressed, taking prescribed medications, and being afraid of waking up and going to work because her immediate manager wasn't appreciative of anything she did. Laura was also working on her PhD thesis and her supervisor was criticizing her. In her eyes, everything seemed hopeless. And even when you listened to her circumstances, it all seemed profoundly negative. I was so moved by her story, about the mental prison she found herself in, but I knew that she needed a deep mindset shift to be able to elevate her vibration, change her fortune, and start attracting abundance and good vibes.

We worked together for six months within the Mastermind, and before we finished, she was feeling happy and sharing her smile with everyone around her. At first, Laura didn't feel like even putting the camera on during the Zoom calls of the Mastermind. Incredible how amazing this process is. Even her clothes changed with more colors and started looking beautiful and engaging. But most importantly was that she finished her PhD thesis and got a new job, doubling her salary and radiating so much positiveness that she is now on the path to a high level of responsibility and leadership. It all started with trusting me, trusting herself, trusting us as a process, as a true journey of transformation.

Similarly, Asma is from Morocco, and was working in London before having to go back to her family house for health issues. She had a good job as a financière in one of the biggest financial institutions in the world. But a health issue coincided with COVID-19 and made her step away from the financial arena for two years. She was feeling depressed, useless, and like no one would care about hiring her because of the two-year gap in her resumé. I worked with Asma intensively for six weeks, and we were able to unlock the power in her that got her into the high-level job she had before her surgery. It helped when she reminded herself that setbacks were temporary, and the downtime she was in a need of played the role of a mental reset, and was the best way to find peace with herself, take care of her health, and honor herself. We worked on her story and her attitude, and she got ready to take on the financial sphere. She was able to land an amazing role at an Investment Bank in London.

Both Laura and Asma were able to turn their sadness and feeling sorry for themselves into powerful opportunities. This is about changing their stories from being the victim to the hero and embarking on a whole different level in their professional journey.

Feeling sad can become your emotional home when you keep it for too long. It will be the normal state you go back to all the time. It almost feels like this is the only thing you know. Some people might even feel that if they're dwelling in sadness, a rescue will come because the universe and the divine will feel sorry for them, and will come to rescue them.

There is no such thing as being rescued by an external force because the force feels your sorrow. You need to put an end to your inner sorrow and emotional distress by shifting your state of mind, by becoming aware that you decide on the journey you want to have in your life. But most important is that by changing your attitude, the environment around you starts shifting and changing.

Finding Meaning

For this phase, I want to share my own story. There's a light way of looking at finding meaning which is reading and studying similar experiences lived by other women or men when they have been able to overcome it. I wrote a book for young girls and young women, showing them that there are countless women before them who have gone through challenges and setbacks but have been able to overcome the difficulties. My book, *African Girl, African Women: How agile, empowered and tech-savvy females will transform the continent... for good*, goes back to history and shares the incredible journey of powerful women who were able to redefine their destiny through their work, research, and contribution to science, academia, medical fields, and business. We stand on the shoulders of hundreds of role models who succeeded before us and crashed the glass ceiling a long time ago.

The book showcases many stories and experiences, and I want to bring up the story of Julia Wainwright to highlight the real-life application of the cycle of grief in changing your life around after a painful episode.

Failure's Reversal of Fortune

Few illustrated the nature of risk better than Julia Wainwright. In the late 1990s, as the early dot-com boom was reaching its peak, Wainwright bought the Pets.com web domain, persuaded Amazon and other VC firms to sink $10.5 million into her new online company, and invested heavily on media—mascots, balloons, public relations, paid advertisements—and built brand recognition among millions of pet owners whose decisions controlled a billion-dollar market. The hype was huge. But there was just one problem. The biggest items, food and cat litter, were heavy, low priced, and expensive to ship. Trying to compete with bricks-and-mortar stores, Pets.com lost money on every transaction. Within two years, in a spectacular fall from power and glory, Wainwright filed for bankruptcy, her company became the embodiment of internet folly, and Pets.com was named one of the greatest dot-com failures in history.

Labeled a failure and publicly humiliated, Wainwright became reclusive, emotionally paralyzed, and psychologically scarred. But after several months she stopped crying and feeling sorry for herself. Instead, she was determined to take over her life and to not let what happened define her, or lead to depression, even death.

Wainwright took responsibility for her own role in the demise of Pets.-com. But with perspective, she also realized that much of the scorn and ridicule she endured was due to her gender. Men were not mocked in the same way; they flopped, shrugged, and moved on. By contrast, Wainwright felt that in the eyes of society she, like females everywhere, was not expected to take the same risks as men, not allowed to experiment against the odds, not permitted to fail. Well, to heck with that. She felt entitled to enjoy the same value. Her risk and failure were merely three or so years in a long career.

So she brushed herself off, set a deadline, got back on her feet, and launched a new startup venture. In contrast to big, heavy, cheap commodities (pet food), her new company, TheRealReal.com, sells small, lightweight, high-quality items like watches and jewelry that have been previously owned, authenticated, and hold their value. It's a sustainable, circular economy of luxury brands. And it's lucrative. Today Wainwright, the sixty year old, is building her new dot-com into a billion dollar 'unicorn,' a story she tells in her book *ReBoot: My Five Life-Changing Mistakes...and How I Moved On*.

Julia is just one example. There are many more who are not as known but their stories are as powerful and might have a lasting impact on you.

Nevertheless, it surely starts giving you meaning for your life and the journey you chose to have.

Acceptance as a First Step to Spirituality

To move to this second phase, it takes more than just understanding and getting inspired by others. You need to be convinced deep inside of you. Because it's about this. The power comes from within you.

This is a way to shift the multitude of negative events into an abundance of positive events. But the "how" was an intriguing part for me. It took two more years after that deep dive research and analysis about the mind and our awareness, and how there's a fine line between the mind, the spinning thoughts, and the spiritual dimension.

The way you elevate and start accepting truly and profoundly what you have gone through. Looking at it as an energy for you to grow and elevate, and understanding the way it pushes you to discover a more profound side of you. This is the start of your spiritual journey.

The best way to explain that is how Michael Singer does in his renowned book, *The Untethered Soul*. In his first chapter, he describes how the elevation happens when you connect with the spiritual dimension. It starts by opening your awareness and observing all the thoughts which are happening in your head. So what is the voice inside of our head? It is what we listen to all the time, and the problem is that we think it's actually us speaking to ourselves.

If you look at anything around you, you start having thoughts about it inside of your head. It could be a bag someone is wearing or shoes. And you start having this conversation with yourself about the color, how it reminds you of something similar you have in your closet. So it feels like we have somebody narrating inside of our head. That's not us, these are our thoughts about the object we focus our attention on. That voice never shuts up, it talks about everything and anything continuously.

Michael Singer developed his interest about the mind and the thinking process when he was a student. He explained the inner dialogue as the psyche not the soul. This was the beginning of his awakening.

Michael Singer's story was the most beautiful explanation of spirituality that spoke to me and triggered such a big shift inside of me. There was a moment which I recall vividly, as I was reading his book, *The Untethered Soul*, again and again and listening to all of his explanations, when I felt a shift. That shift was in my energy. I was the same, but something deep inside of me was awakened.

Singer with his spiritual side was able to survive the toughest corporate scandal in modern history. He reached multi-millions with his tech company. Being a CEO, he was faced with accusations due to fraudulent behaviors happening in his company.

He was able to stay centered through the process despite the injustice, accusations, auditing, and the news around it. The way Singer handled that was by elevating spirituality and becoming "closer to God" in his own words.

It represents the awareness of the thought and the voice inside of our head, where our consciousness resides and that's who we are. This was the open door for Michael Singer and for many who matured and elevated in relationship with the mind.

This is the road to the spiritual path, to understanding that you are a spiritual being.

You know you're not the thoughts because you are watching them. Just like when you are having nightmares and you are aware of them happening and watching yourself being disturbed by them. They are thoughts, they are not you.

So how can you start to separate yourself from your thoughts? That is the key. Because when you do that, you become free from your thoughts and all the strings which are attached to them.

That's the beginning of your spirituality. When you are able to separate what you are not but what you really are.

If you continue to be involved in the mind, you get lost in it. The main questions to ask as you elevate in your spiritual path are: Who are you? Who is the voice inside of you?

When Oprah Winfrey asked Michael Singer, "Who took that path to spiritual elevation, who are you?"

He answered, "At this stage of my growth, I am the one that is here (pointing to his head) who notices the thought come up, who notices the emotions in our heart, and who sees whoever is in front of my senses. I am the seer. I am the one who sees."

Witnessing the thoughts passing by as you zoom out, you start watching your thoughts and the mental activities. You disconnect. Your thoughts become something that you are experiencing and watching, and not something that you are.

The secret to finding joy and inner peace is illustrated through Michael Singer and how he was able, with his deep spirit, to survive a corporate scandal and lose his multi-million business. Michael Singer was already on a spiritual path, and his challenge helped him grow even more and become a spiritual guru and a reference in the understanding of the mind and elevation.

Spiritual growth happens when there is only one person inside of us ... not a part that is scared, and another part of you that is protecting the part that is scared. When the two parts are integrated and in harmony, that is the moment where we start feeling enlightened and relaxed. At that moment, when problems show up, the first reaction is to relax and lean away from the noise the mind is making around the problems.

That is the growth process that takes consistency, perseverance, and many days.

We always have two clear choices when faced with problems and over-whelming, scary thoughts and negative energies. When it starts, you can lean in and get involved. Or you can relax and lean away from it, you start to take space. You will realize that this is the best thing you could have ever done.

I applied that in my own life and I helped several women through their own leveling up.

During my own professional turmoil, I wanted to be connected to that part of me that is spiritual, and I couldn't find a better way to explain what it means than Michael Singer's thorough and profound under-standing on how I can elevate and start seeing innocence in those who hurt me, those who pointed the finger at me, and those who betrayed me according to my own dictionary of understanding.

This is the power of God when you let it guide you. The power of the universe. The infinite intelligence that connects us to the cosmos and all its wonders.

A lot of spiritual gurus seclude themselves and go on without talking to anyone, focusing on meditation and shutting off the noise in their head. Being a mother of four, I couldn't possibly conceive leaving them behind to go look for myself. I had to integrate that into my daily way of being. Adapting to the existing circumstances and elevating through the process I created and am able to share with hundreds, thousands, and yes millions of women. Showing them their own path to elevation, to connecting with the bigger force and to creating the harmonious elevation of their soul.

You lean away from the mess that the mind is doing, to amplify what is happening. This is so true. I know that feeling of reaching silence and stillness around you, when before it was absolutely impossible to quiet the highways of thoughts in the mind. The seventy thousand thoughts that rush in and out of your head, spinning over and over. When you start having spiritual experiences, you realize that the majority of problems are passing by. You don't need medication anymore to reach that state when you master the zooming out and reach that spiritual awakening. This is the moment when it becomes obvious what needs to be done next.

All of this makes you understand that you, me, we are all spiritual beings in a human body. You are a spiritual being, living a human experience. And whatever you go through pushes you to get closer to that understanding.

Once you truly embrace that, that will be the beginning of the road to spirituality. The ability to separate what you are from what you are not.

If you continue to choose to be completely involved in the thoughts and the mind, and you get lost in your beliefs and the different ideas that cross the mind, the spiritual elevation does not happen.

Going back to Michael Singer, the way to open your gateway to spirituality is by asking the questions:

- Who am I?
- Who is that voice in my head?

For me, "How am I?" became more and more clear, as I was maturing and strengthening my mental state through the challenges and the experience. That is the moment when I realized that my calling is to become a catalyst for every woman to help her power up no matter how tough the circumstances are.

When you understand who you are, you learn the ability to disconnect from your thoughts. You start understanding that you are a spiritual being when you understand that you are not the thoughts. Because you are actually watching the thoughts so you cannot be them at the same time.

When you analyze any situation: Are you going to go through the situation feeling sorry for yourself and what happened to you? Or are you going to let the situation pull out from your heart whatever is left of grudges from the past and of bitterness? This is your decision to make. When you embody the true understanding of what a life of growth and evolution means, you will step up spiritually and energetically.

The only way is to be willing to let go of the psychological self, your identity. In order to be who you truly are, you must let go of who you think you are. The old version of you must die so that the new *you* can be reborn.

To be reborn, as you let that go, you use spirituality and you meditate so that you have the calmness and the higher frequencies. You will lean away from the mess that the mind is doing to amplify and over exaggerate what is happening. Then you reach a state of well-being that is freedom. Because the true freedom is freedom from yourself and from your thoughts.

Removing Your Inner Thorn

Imagine that you have a thorn that's pressing directly on a nerve so that anything that touches you hurts you. A perfect way to describe it as used by Michael Singer in his book and his interviews.

When you have people who remind you of your issues and problems, you have two choices—you can either avoid anything in your life that touches that thorn or you can take it out.

I want to share the story of Ingrid, who joined the program after coming out of a painful divorce with her husband. Ingrid was going through not only a whole readaptation in her life but having to learn how to co-exist with her ex-husband at work because they both worked in the same institution. Every time she found him in a meeting, her emotions took over and she lost her voice and wasn't able to carry out her work efficiently. The situation was impacting not only her private life but her professional life as well.

This image helped her tremendously. Because of the pain of the divorce, she had many thorns in her, and each time she heard his name or saw him in a corridor, she felt fearful and unsafe.

The thorns were in, and no one and nothing could touch them. The question was how to create a life that would not twist those thorns.

But there was a way to remove all these thorns. The only way to do it was to understand the mind and how to shift it, but even more importantly, how to realign to spirituality.

Disturbance happens inside. What is happening is irritating your thorn. Those events will show you.

This is why you need to learn how to deal with the disturbance and how to remove the thorn. By elevating, we let go of the grudges from the past and we are less and less affected by what comes from it.

This is how we use our problem as a way forward in our spiritual path.

So what do you do when you feel disturbance? You relax. You recognize the emotion that is triggered and let it pass. You become more aware of yourself and of what is happening in you.

There is so much joy and spiritual strength when you let any thorn be removed. The best way to shift this and not let negative thoughts in your head is by being aware of them and changing them into positive ideas and thoughts. Mantra also helps by repeating a cheering sentence and a positive thought.

Creating Something New

The last phase is about you being reborn. Recreating yourself and redefining the role that you have to play during your lifetime.

There is a general law that is: create or disintegrate. Every living thing is bound by this law. When you look at a plant, you will never see a plant stagnating at the same step. A flower cannot stay the same way forever; it either blossoms or disintegrates and dies. No flower or plant stagnates, keeping the same color and the same size day after day. The same thing with humans; you need to be in the process of creation and cognitive activity that push you to progress, so that you can feel alive, and you can be alive. Otherwise, you will not only lose your momentum, but you will be feeling that you are disintegrating. We have a desperate need for growth and evolution as human beings. When you understand that life is best experienced as a journey of growth and evolution, you will express a deep gratitude from every step taken and be ready for what is coming next.

Creating something new is giving a new breath to your life, and to do so, it's important to define a purpose and a mission that are aligned with your new maturity. After having gone through the difficult experience and through the different phases, you are able to see by now that you have a power in you that you didn't know you had before. You are also feeling a new energy and a new push to recreate yourself. Just like a phoenix bursting out of the ashes, flying out, seeking new ways to show others what is possible. Rising for your children, your family, your loved ones, or simply for yourself and the love of life.

At that moment, it's important to define an objective that is so big in terms of its context that it will be hard to dismiss it.

It helps to remember and to understand the importance of broadening your perspectives if you keep the focus and not sabotage yourself when you see that you're not achieving small objectives with tight deadlines you gave yourself.

We set goals to stay focused, to know where we are going, and to remind ourselves of the possibilities and give meaning to our life.

You will be able to go through this cycle with more ease and find your path towards your success and positive opportunities. This mission will become your context. The very large sphere that holds your goals, objectives, and all of your aspirations. By making your context large, it will overwhelm you, and your mission becomes your fuel to take over the whole space you created for yourself from that context.

When you create a strong belief in your mission, you can make it so powerful and aligned with who you really are. Because when you keep your goals and objectives broad, they become your legacy. This way you will not get into a self-sabotaging mood as soon as something doesn't go your way. And you will be able to zoom out from the difficulties by looking at the larger picture.

Holding on to the Larger Context

When you see yourself advancing and something happens to pull you back again. When you see yourself progressing, and an event brings you back to less than where you started. The question is how do you keep on believing when things get overwhelming?

Where do you get the strength from again? Where do you get the inspiration from again? How do you create that push again?

When you feel everything is pulling you back. That vortex of negative thoughts is here. A spiral of negative stimulation of thoughts you visited time and time again, will be taking you to the darkest places. But you won't let it happen this time. I know how it feels, you say "no" this time. Because you have gone through the cycle of grief once, you are not going to go there again. So, if you get trapped again, trust that you will break free the same way, or probably better than last time.

If it takes time, let it be. If it takes the pain and hurt, let it be. If it takes struggle, let it be.

Trust how the bigger power is taking away what was left in you within that egocentric space. Surrender to that energy that is pushing you to grow more powerful.

You will rise again. You will feel the rebirth again and again. You will use your genius and your inner power. What you have learned from all these experiences makes you grow in maturity and wisdom. You will master how to collapse time between cycles as you navigate through life. This is when broadening your vision and making your mission so big creates your larger context. This way your journey will hold many stories, many ups, many downs, and many cycles.

By embracing every part of your journey, you will find beauty in suffering and struggling. Because, every emotion teaches us something new and valuable. All it takes is to hold on tight to your context and to your vision, as you learn how to collapse time towards your biggest dream.

---

1. www.balmethod.com

My Workbook - Chapter 3

What did I learn from the hardest experience in my life?

What will I do differently now?

What can I share to teach others my wisdom?

What is my mission and how do I define my context?

4

Unleash Your Driving Force

Where did I get my power from when I took the French engineering school competition with hundreds of students for them to pick less than ten students and got in? Where did I get my strength from to get accepted to Harvard and be honored with a doctorate? Where did I get the power to work with the World Bank Vice President and President, and be so appreciated as a young professional? Where did I get that strength to become an economic advisor to Morocco's Prime Minister? Where did I get the power to be a mother of four beautiful children?

I had to remember who I was. I needed to recall those moments when I felt glorious. They were lost somewhere. Day after day, I was putting the seed of strength in my subconscious mind. Watering it with gratitude from nature, from the love of my children and my husband, and from keeping the momentum with discipline. And all the energetics are woven in the process.

We go through different phases in our life. There are moments when it is about working hard. Being present as an executive, a corporate, a manager, or a leader. About being ready to share value, to provide a service. These moments are fed by the force of life and are also a source of the force of life. This is how we build connections, how we show up and carry on no matter what.

And of course, there are also times when you just want to enjoy who you are and be in that moment. All you long to do is to take care of yourself by just sitting in front of the sea, the mountain, in the forest, or simply in a cozy corner of your home. A moment to remember who you are, and to do absolutely nothing. Enjoying that "feeling well because all is okay." These downtime moments are as important as the heavy-duty ones. They ground you and center you. They help you remember why you are doing all the work in the first place, and they help you feel that you are living your life in the present and enjoying every moment.

This should make you feel like you are taking a little vacation whenever you feel the urge for a break. This is the way you reach the work-life balance we all thrive for. It is adopting a lifestyle you don't want to retire from.

On a bigger scale, we have phases where we reach success and great achievements, and phases where we are faced with challenges, obstacles, and difficulties.

I have been through these two types of phases, and I know for sure that when you are in that lowest phase, it is hard to get yourself back up, but you surely can. It takes resilience, perseverance, and most importantly the right state of mind combined with discipline.

That discipline is not about work at first. That discipline is about loving yourself, caring for who you are and your accomplishments, and forgiving yourself for anything from that hurtful past.

Then you reach phase six from the cycle of grief as you get to that time when you can recreate yourself and thrive again in whatever direction you choose. These are the cycles that make the big "Circle of Life." The ups and downs. That circle will always make you win when you keep on believing, when you hold on to your faith. It constantly makes you stand back up when you get aligned with the divine and the infinite intelligence.

The strength in you can be triggered when you understand the mind and the realm of energetics. Because there is a light inside of you. That light will become your own, become for everything you do in your life, and it will guide you through your intuition, creativity, and deep channeling.

The inner power is infinite when it connects with the understanding of the divine, the infinite intelligence, the universe, and the cosmic. This inner power can be demonstrated scientifically. Being an engineer, my brain functions with a very structured logic, and if I'm able to confirm that everything around us is related to energy, it is because I studied the science behind it. Within the science field, we find a very fine line between all the understanding of light, quantum physics, and the cosmic and spirituality. When you grasp this part, your life changes.

I borrow motivational and inspirational lines from movies and songs. No show presents the Circle of Life as perfectly as Disney's *The Lion King*.

> "There is more to see than can ever be seen,
>
> And more to do than can ever be done."

The Circle of Life is about infinite possibilities, infinite wealth, and infinite power.

We Are Waves of Energy

There is so much power inside each one of us it can be used to illuminate a whole city. When you understand quantum and nuclear physics, you understand the incredible power we carry in our bodies. Our body is made of atoms and electrons, and everything that science is using to demonstrate, confirm, and convince you that we are waves of energy.

When you take an ultrasound of your body, you radiate waves of energy. When you integrate this, you are able to grasp the level of power you have in you. That power can take you to create incredible wealth and success in your life. Things become accessible, and what seemed hard and overwhelming before, seen from this new perspective, becomes incredible.

In fact, these waves of energy mirror the magnetic field that centers out from our heart. Thus, energy is evaluated in terms of vibration. Vibration represents a frequency in physics and on the Hertz scale. And from a human understanding, frequency, vibration, energy, they simply represent our emotions. This is why what we feel is what we see more of. This is one of the most powerful notions woven through this book.

Einstein said, "Everything is energy and that's all there is to it. Match the frequency of the reality you want and you cannot help but get that reality. It can be no other way. This is not Philosophy. This is Physics."

From a human perspective, matching the frequency of what you want in life means matching your current emotions with the emotions of the goal achieved. It means feeling all the gratitude and the happiness you would feel just as if you have already arrived at your life destination. Because emotions are the mirror of the level of vibration where you are and the energy frequency you stand on.

So when you wake up and feel that you don't have enough energy or you don't have the energy to take on your day, in reality, it means that you prefer to dwell in your negative thinking, feeling that life is too hard and too overwhelming. You can change what you expect, by changing the way you see things.

This is how changing your results and what you have in your life starts with your state of mind. In other words, it starts with the level of emotional maturity and alignment with how you want to feel and celebrating the achievements you want to see happening in your life. This is why there is such a strong emotional force in you that represents *life*.

The Emotional Force of Life

Unleashing your driving force starts with the emotional force. It's about finding new beliefs and creating new realities for yourself. Because as soon as you shift your thoughts and beliefs, it changes everything in you.

This is why we don't accumulate knowledge for the sake of accumulating. It is what you do with that knowledge that matters and how you use it to thrive in your life. The opportunity is there and now it's important to put it to work.

Let your learning lead to action. Then you can create a life you didn't dream about.

Success is not about what you do, it's about what you feel when you are doing what you do. Your emotional intelligence is overriding everything else. When your emotions are too high, you cannot think properly. You need to be able to ground yourself before making a decision. A lot of people make decisions they regret later when they do it from a space of anger, stress, fear, anxiety, sadness, or shame.

The emotions are the first thing that precede you when you enter a room, when you communicate and when you handle your business. This is why you need to be super clear around your emotions for you to thrive and for you to lead. The number one skill of a leader is the skill to influence the thoughts, feelings, and actions of another person. The way we influence is by using emotional intelligence. This is a skill you need to master as a good manager, a good parent, a good business owner, or a good friend. You need to learn how to influence. To do that, you need to start by influencing the person that matters most, and that is you.

Therefore, if you are not in a position to be able to influence yourself to do certain things, if you are not exercising this ability in yourself, you cannot be a leader. It comes down to the way you think.

To be able to discover that on your own, you need to find out what are the things that are influencing you, so that you can understand what shapes people's lives. Most of these forces that influence people are invisible.

Just like radiation, electricity, and magnetic fields are invisible, the emotional human force is the ultimate resource and the most powerful.

Everything in life comes from emotion. We justify our actions and circumstances intellectually, but it all comes from emotion first.

So when you know that you are able to create an incredible life, but you don't do it, it is because there is a blockage at the emotional level. And that blockage is about fear.

You need to be able to coexist with fear and doubt, and use them to fuel the life force in you.

That's the moment when you need to recalibrate and let faith guide you. You do that by understanding the signals. The signals from your brain are always about warning and primitive survival mode. So you have continuous thoughts and warnings. "What if I fail? What's going to happen? What will people think? How can I handle it?"

So if I focus on fear, I will be experiencing more of it. This is why it's essential to learn how to direct the focus and not let the fear take control.

What you feed with your thoughts will flourish. If it is fear, it will grow. If it is what you desire, it will thrive.

Thus, emotional intelligence is the hardest part. When emotions are high, intelligence is low. This is when people say things they don't mean. People say things out of fear and make decisions out of pain. They regret those decisions later. What we want to experience most in life is to feel that we are okay, and there is nothing dangerous or scary around us. This is why the most important thing is to create circumstances that make us feel comfortable, and that we are safe.

The only thing to do is to be in alignment with who you are, what you believe, and what you want. Instead of trying to override fear, when you come from a space of worthiness and abundance, the fear becomes the fuel you need to push yourself, to try for more, to create and to grow more empowered.

Regardless of the external circumstances, the level of maturity and strength of your emotional intelligence gets tested when you need to stay in alignment. You could be having the most powerful day and something external happens to you that makes you angry, sad, or stressed. At that moment, your emotions are triggered and your intelligence goes down. So you lose yourself if you're not able to lock your super power by staying grounded and calm on the inside. It can be hard at the beginning, but the more you practice your ability to remain in a state of alignment and feeling grounded, the more you will become in charge of you and you will start feeling your super power inside of you. This is why you need to be and become the person you want to be.

Before taking action and doing, you need to believe in yourself and truly be that person you are seeking to be. These two steps come before the leading, which is the moment when you are having the abundance and the recognition you are working towards.

The second phase will not matter if you are not feeling good. You don't feel good when you are not truly believing.

When you are genuinely in that state, your inner power becomes the energy that you radiate. At that moment, people will become magnetized to your energy and who you are.

Emotional intelligence is everything. Otherwise, you will feel stuck, stressed, and angry.

Doing is intuitive when it comes from a true belief and being in the most powerful emotional state. The impact of the doing is incomparable to when you aren't in the appropriate state of mind. Because at the moment, the flood gate opens for you in the universe of alignment. Therefore, working hard and taking action won't matter if you aren't feeling good about it. At that moment, you need to go back to your emotional state and shift your mindset.

It took me many experiences and magical surprises in my life to understand that my personal power is a total reflection of my emotional state. It becomes a magnet that pulls things that are in alignment.

Therefore, when people get emotionally triggered and lose their temper, they have no personal power. What makes a difference in people is how they keep their power inside and always communicate and act from a space of alignment. The recipe of abundance and fulfillment is based on your alignment, your emotional mastery, and how you are able to translate that inner power into the physical world through your communication, your actions, and all your doings.

Finally, what creates power is when people are drawn to your energy. They are magnetized because your energetic signature is clear, stable, and positive. Consequently, the stronger the force you send out to the world, the more you magnetize the world. This is why it's so important to protect and nurture it. You can protect your energy by what you choose and decide to think about, speak about, feel, and work on. And of course, by who you surround yourself with and the environment that you create around you. This is the most powerful knowledge you can master to tap into your driving force.

The Law of Attraction

You, me, us. We are vibrational beings, with an energetic, electro-magnetic frequency. That is the signal you emit when people are around you. They feel it like a vibe. We are made of waves of energy. It's all scientifically proven. By looking into the microscope lens, the tiniest cell in our body is made of the smallest vibrating particles. So everything is moving. The studies and teaching of Michael Bernard Beckwith present a thorough and detailed explanation of the Law of Attraction. In his words: "When we lift our vibration to what we want to experience, it has to be first on the vibratory level and it shows up and manifests in our life."

This means that if you hold on to hurtful and negative emotions, complaining and nagging about everything from your past, if someone did something bad to you and you hold on to that, it will not change the way they feel about you. Even if you are hoping that it will make them feel guilty and come back to apologize. This will not happen. All that it does is that it makes your vibration stuck in the lowest level, attracting more of the same so that your feelings remain low. This means holding on to anger, grudges, and animosity will hamper your success and will make reaching your objectives seem too hard and so far away.

So clearly explained by Beckwith: "You cannot have what you are not willing to become vibrationally. If you get it, you lose it." This explains when people get their dream job, but they lose it. Or people meet a partner of their dreams, but cannot keep a good relationship.

People need to be vibrationally aligned with what they are looking to receive. We do manage to manipulate it a bit, but it cannot last. For you to receive that level of joy, happiness, success, wealth, and everything you dream about, you need to align with that very frequency. As vibratory beings, when we align with the frequency we are looking for, we radiate that frequency. We become a magnet to what we are looking to attract in our life.

When you are able to radiate the frequency of joy, love, or peace, it will show up in your life as you attract more joy, love, and peace of mind. It isn't about attracting, it's about embodying the changes in you, the high vibration in you.

I experienced that personally when I was drawn into the problems in one of my companies which was in charge of structuring and managing eight and nine figure management funds. I was seeing only the dark from those problems and dwelling in what I was worried about what could come, what could happen. Anxiety became the normal state.

I understood that I wasn't asking the right questions. Dwelling on why this happened to me. Why have they done this to me? Recreating all the moments over and over in my head was amplifying the anxiety, stress, fear of the unknown, and the threat from it all.

It took me one fraction of a second. Come back home scattered, lost, hurt, and bitter about the cruelty of people and of life. Tears in my eyes. Knot in my throat. Pain and hurt inside of me. Every part of my body felt heavy. I couldn't find calmness. Thousands and thousands of thoughts spinning in my head.

I came home, saw my three daughters having chocolate milk in the kitchen, and I looked at them. I knew at that moment that life had prepared me for something else that didn't include feeling sorry for myself. That something else did not include dwelling on problems and drawing them in. That something else meant recreation. Meant looking for strength because my daughters didn't deserve this. I was their hope, their role model, their everything. Their dream for a great life. Their dream for a future of happiness, joy, glory, and celebrations.

It took me a second to paint that image so vividly in my head that it became my reminder every day. I have gone through all that I have achieved in my life to let something or someone destroy it all for me? No. Never.

This was my unshakable decision to rise back up from the ashes just like a phoenix. Music, stories, and discipline helped me.

I had to work on myself to love myself while on my own. I needed to take a small step to elevate my vibration. My scientific mind knew that the moment I made a decision I was turning my life around. So I focused on studying energetics and vibration. My connection with the Law of Attraction has always been there in my life, since the moment I made it to the top of my class from an early age because I made that my goal. I did the same when I was playing piano competition in my early teens. I knew the power of focus and hard work.

But, what happened to my life for it to attract such a challenge? People would refer to it as a failure ... I referred to it as a setback, as a challenge.

At that moment, my profound mission became to raise my vibration and to rise up emotionally. It was my own healing journey.

The healing process took days, weeks, and months. I was making baby steps filled with gratitude and love. I knew the power of gratitude. I started with my garden. I got a plant, another plant, flowers, and hortensia. Every day I saw them growing, I was grateful. They mirrored my inside. The garden became beautiful and every morning I was grateful about it. Because you grow what you plant—either in nature or inside of you, within your subconscious mind.

After two to three months, flowers were blooming, my gratitude grew, and I found love.

I was looking at myself for the first time without a voice in my head spewing contempt for me and everything I'd gone through. I felt the love for having made the decision, started to feel the pride for perseverance, for finding resilience when I thought I had no more of it. I disconnected from toxic news, messages, and information. I disconnected from family members or friends who felt sorry for me, from those who didn't fit my recreation trend and mood. I didn't want to be in the victim's emotional space and did not want to be justifying anything to anyone. Not even about why I made my unshakable decision. I wasn't ready, I was creating that protective shield. So, I deliberately focused on my children and my husband, strengthening the love, affection, and nurturing of my family.

It took me discipline and a profound studying of the psychology of the mind, combined with a deeper understanding of energetics and spirituality.

To me, this was a connection with God, prayer, meditation, yoga, and openness to infinite intelligence. The power of the universe connected me with my deep belief in God and faith. I remember how I was in the dark, lost between who I knew I was before, the person that was so scared by the avalanche of problems and blame, and who I am growing to become. But I didn't know who I was becoming.

Until one day, I was changed. I cannot say exactly what day. But I knew that morning that I grew spiritually and emotionally, and I matured by disconnecting from the problems and the worry around me. That day, I wasn't feeling the sting inside of me as deep when someone or something reminded me of that corporate episode. I even became grateful for the event because it changed me. It gave me a deep understanding of what it means to feel reborn. And what it takes to unleash the power in you and find the strength when no one thought you would.

It all starts with love—love for myself, love for you, and love for us. Looking back, I now realize you need to start by loving yourself when you are by yourself. Otherwise, you will be taking from others to make yourself happy and it's never enough.

The questions that I was asking were not the "Why me?" anymore. They became: What did I learn from it? What is the wisdom that comes from it? What is the growth that I am experiencing from it?

These questions are so empowering. They surely brought something more powerful and more aligned with who I truly am inside of me. But one thing I know for sure, my story is not a victim story. My story is an empowering and inspiring one. It brings hope, it brings possibility to everyone. If I'm able to transform my life, to grow from having lost everything and find that strength in me to bring the dignity, the honor back in the deepest part of myself, you surely can. Building wealth in a more gratifying way, so that it is for me, for you, for us.

At that moment, I discovered such a profound sense of purpose and service. I had it before for sustainable development and a world free of poverty, but now my mission was more specific, clear, and integrated with my daily professional and personal activities.

Answering the: Why am I here? What is the service that I am here to give to the planet? Why was I born to go through all these experiences?

The answer was so clear to me. My purpose and my service is to help every woman to find love, to find peace, to unleash her power to create wealth and make an impact.

This is how my mission is so unique to me, the same way your purpose and your mission will be unique to you.

That was the second powerful moment when I felt I was different. Something had changed deep inside of me. I will not be the same ever again. So much about growing inside of me and about understanding abundance. This is the spiritual leveling up and getting ready to access infinite possibilities.

Finally, when you ask for help from the divine, from the infinite intelligence, it will show up. It will come. When you deeply, truly understand the power of frequency and get ready to unleash it, it will show up.

Therefore, make your driving force, your mission, your vision, and your context bigger than any problem or challenge you can encounter. Instead of spending time asking, "Why me?" Ask, "What if something amazing shows up? What if I can grow more, impact more, create more, and attract more wealth, joy, love, and peace of mind?"

Start by Starving the Problems

Reality is far from being that simple. Because when you find yourself overwhelmed with responsibilities and problems, they absorb every part of your brain. They pile up and make you feel like you are blocked by a huge wall, creating a terror barrier, or you are stuck in a strong storm.

In those cases, you are faced with two options. The first direction is when the storm carries you in the vicious circle of anxiety, stress, and feeling like hiding in a rabbit hole of depression. The second direction is when you power up, display your resilience, and become invincible by focusing on the solutions and starving the problems.

Problems build up when you feed them with continuous worries and thoughts. However, when you starve them, you make them look and feel smaller. This means that you shouldn't let problems take over and absorb all your energy. Just the opposite. You should put things in perspective and choose strategically to focus on solutions and on how to grow despite the hurdles. Often, challenges are there to show you another path where you can thrive and create more success. You just need to trust the process and have faith.

Stay Strong No Matter What

I have been a professional, a hard-working woman, a strategist, and an overachiever my whole life, because I was programmed that way. This had become my normal personality throughout the years.

I started at the World Bank in Washington right after my Harvard PhD. I traveled the world in my twenties and early thirties working on development strategies for countries and remote regions to reduce poverty, to bring the basic infrastructure and make a difference in people's lives.

Then I worked in the government, in the public sector, and in the private sector reaching executive and leadership roles, before becoming a strategic entrepreneur.

But the best part of my professional journey is being a mother of four beautiful children. Because caring and giving true love continuously with no expectation is the most beautiful thing you can do. And it is the most sustainable source of fuel and energy which helps you carry on.

That part has been my savior when my professional life was going through the ups and downs of a drama movie!

Perhaps not that part alone, as I needed a strong resilience. That is the time when the warrior inside of me needed to come out. Because, when you need to rebuild yourself, you need to embrace several personalities, and the challenge is to find them inside of you.

This is the reason why I created the BAL Method[1] in a way that helps women Believe in themselves and in their talent and gifts, to structure a strategic plan to take Action in reaching their goals, and to Lead with their inner power.

The inner power is stronger than the circumstantial power. The latter comes from the good education, good job, a respected position, a family that supports you when growing up and all the support you get from an outside circumstance. While the inner power is from within. It is the power that you need to create the circumstances when you don't find them. It is the one that you use to stand confident and empowered if you get overwhelmed with the circumstantial power itself. The inner power is triggered when you are on top of your emotional intelligence. What makes a difference among leaders, empowered leaders and great leaders is how much they are aware of their feelings and how they master their emotions so that their intelligence remains intact no matter what.

By connecting the dots for women, the BAL Method helps them create wealth and make a sustainable impact around them. And most importantly, when you master and understand when and how to use the four personalities, it becomes possible to thrive no matter what and to turn your vision into a reality.

Master the Four Universal Archetypes

There are four types of personalities which play an important role in influencing your behavior and your state of mind. They are known as the Universal Archetypes.

When you master them, the only job you will have going forward is to know which one to use and when:

- The *Magician*: This is your intuition and the unique gifts you have inside of you.
- The *Warrior*: That is the infinite power inside of you, which can take you to anywhere you want in your life.
- The *Lover*: That is all the love in you. That is why you need to fill it up by loving yourself truly first to find what to give.

- The *Sovereign*: This is the one that deserves and commands respect from you and from everyone.

When you feel lost ... always remember that you have these four personalities in you. When there's something missing in your puzzle of life, keep these personalities handy. There are techniques that you can use, combined with discipline and repetitive actions, that put you back on track no matter what. It will make you feel ready each time to use the techniques and tools to unleash the leader inside of you and turn your life around!

There are two ways of coping with difficulties and challenges in life—either you let them control you or you take control of them. If the second was that simple, we would all be standing in control of what is happening in our lives all the time. However, when you master the four personalities you have inside of you, you will start feeling more in charge and in tune with your inner peace.

The Magician

When you are able to raise your level of vibration, you reach a higher consciousness in your mind. At that moment, you can attract incredible things in your life because you radiate such high energy that you become in tune with the Law of Attraction. To me, that is what I call and feel is magic. When you tune into that power, you become the Magician in your life.

Thus, the Magician in you is about your intuition and the unique gifts you have inside of you. When you are aware of them and you know how to let them guide you, you can make the impossible possible.

This magical personality is the essence of life. This is when you let your inner light guide you. It happens when you start listening to your intuition. The more you elevate from a spiritual perspective, the more you become in harmony with the universal laws. These universal laws include the Law of Attraction, which opens up infinite possibilities and is the portal to see your dreams become reality.

Feeling the magic doesn't feel unfamiliar, it's all part of our childhood years. Just like that moment when you step into the Magic Kingdom at Walt Disney World. Something changes in you. It feels so familiar, like you have always been in that magical space. It's a space that we know so well.

Here is how it works! Your subconscious mind takes you back to childhood, where everything used to feel safe, easy, happy, and simple.

I know how it feels because I took my children as an excuse to go back to the magical park.

But in reality, I was probably the one manifesting those very moments and found myself in the middle of sparks, colors, music, and beautiful magic. I couldn't find a better place to celebrate the creation of the BAL Method and to celebrate the hundred women who have seen their life transforming through this method. I could not be more thrilled, and proud of my own transformation. Becoming a real manifestation of magic in your life. From coming back after such a difficult professional experience, I used those challenges to find a power in me I didn't know I had. After visualizing a happy and magical moment, where my children were so proud of me in my morning routine, as I was working on elevating my own vibrations. The morning we stepped into Disney World, it was a moment I lived every day for the whole year, and finding myself in the middle of it, came to confirm that there is that Magician in you.

We are often needing to go back to childhood magic more than our own children because we starve for those beautiful, happy moments from our childhood. Finding that magical space is a walk down memory lane, going back and remembering that happiness is in each one of you.

There have been moments of happiness throughout your life, and particular during childhood. But you let go of them, or rather you forgot about them. You replace them with the challenges, the difficulties, the worries about the unforeseen future, and the weight of the hard work that needs to be done for every aspect of life. So, it feels very heavy. All of this gets amplified as the years unfold with more challenges and responsibilities.

But the child in you has never left. That child constantly needs reassurance and to feel safe. This is why you need to play that role for yourself. Otherwise you will look for evidence around you to reassure you by holding on to relationships, becoming dependent on them, and asking for help and guidance in every decision you need to make. At that moment, you tend to believe in unreal solutions that promise quick wins. On top of that, using vanity metrics even though they can never last because they do not mirror reality.

So, beware of trusting whoever promises an easy ride as you will get disappointed and even more frustrated. But you know better now. What you actually need is to understand how the mind functions and what the child in you needs to hear. The child in you has never left. That's fun, creative, beautiful, and truly amazing. Be grateful for everything you have become to be able to truly raise your vibration. Be appreciative of what you have become through the years. Be proud of your accomplishments no matter how small they feel in your eyes. You have perfection and magic in you. Tap into them and grab every happy moment from your past and your current life. You have them in you. Let them be your norm, and carry on to have a magical day.

By becoming your own reassurance for yourself and believing in yourself, you will increase your trust in the process as your faith grows about how things will work out no matter what.

It all starts by visualizing the dream life you're looking for, stepping into your imagination, and embracing your magical dream.

Magic starts when you surrender to the possibilities and feed your day with positive thoughts and positive energy. Continuously raising your vibration. The Magician in you is the one who understands the power in you and how you use your emotional power to guide and to transform you into a magnet to all the good things in your life. Master the emotional power in you and you will feel in alignment. Being in alignment with it means that your thoughts, your emotions, and your actions are all the same. Your emotional energy is the magic you use to be, to communicate, and to attract material things into your life. When you start a conversation, that energy precedes you. When you enter a room, your energy speaks before you do. People feel your energy. This is why that Magician works without you needing to express yourself or to do anything.

This is why you need to ensure that your energy is aligned with the high vibration you want to attract in your life.

The Warrior

Where is the Warrior in you? Where is that personality that protects you? That comes from your uniqueness, from knowing that you have been created in this universe for a reason. Nothing happens haphazardly. It is all synchronized with the cosmic power that makes everything fit in its place, just as if it was a huge puzzle for greatness that you created out of your life.

That animal side of you, that protective instinct, how does it show up? The superwoman in you and the superman in you. You can trigger them in a way that is unbelievably effective and impactful.

That is the infinite power inside of you. It will take you anywhere you want in life. The Warrior in you will help you overcome all the obstacles you encounter on your path towards your dream goal, no matter how hurtful they might be.

Just like my mothering instinct, when I wanted to protect my four children from having a mother who was hurt and scattered. An animal instinct triggers the hint of the superwoman in me. The hint of a phoenix getting ready to be reborn. Bringing the Warrior out is taking over your life. Becoming in control of what is happening to you, you will feel empowered. I saw it like Xena the Warrior, or Wonder Woman. I also found the spark in the Netflix series, *Queen of the South*. That image of Teresa, the leading role, who has gone through so much pain and suffering to become the queen of narcotraffic with a drive to legitimize her business. Her war against mafias and gangsters was triggered by the image of herself in a white dress coming out of her black limousine. While imprisoned by a gangster, she told herself that she would look back as she rose as the queen of the biggest cartel and would feel proud of what she had gone through and how she was able to survive it all.

This is why we insist on women empowerment so much. It's to help women get their Warrior out and ready to win. It has the same impact on men as well. But let's dive into the meaning of empowerment and the triggering of the Warrior.

So what does it mean in reality to feel empowered?

When I talk about empowerment, what I really mean is taking back your authority. This means you sign an open authorization to yourself where you allow yourself to be in charge of your day, your decisions, your work, your life, and your happiness.

This might feel obvious when you first read it, but in many cases, we get caught up in a habitual way of being and of doing business. When you look deeper, and you analyze how things are moving and functioning, you realize that you are not fully in charge of all of those aspects.

It might even feel hard to be all of that at the same time. That is the moment when you find all the perfect justifications and reasons why being in charge is complicated ... or even impossible. You think to yourself that it can wait 'til tomorrow, next week, next month, or even next year.

Because it feels complicated to change something in that perfect, habitual way of being. But this is how and why only one percent of the population in the world has ninety-six percent of the wealth. This is why it's time to power up, be in charge of your life, and get the Warrior out. That Warrior will help you create the circumstances when you don't see them.

Changing the physiology of your body will bring you the stamina and the energy you need to power up. This is why exercising is so powerful, it generates the hormone you need in your body to feel the drive and to feel that you can. A lot of motivational speakers integrate moving the body and dancing in their routine to pump everyone up and to get the adrenaline going and the feeling of empowerment. But this doesn't last. As soon as the event is over, your normal life weaves itself back to its place if you don't set up a mechanism to change once and for all. That mechanism is a process, is the discipline to get yourself into new vibes on a daily basis. To integrate a daily routine of gratitude and visualization of where you are going in your life. The Warrior in you will become the action taker, strategic planner, and the one who gets things done.

Finally, the Warrior is about the doing, the taking action, and the perseverance no matter what blockage, challenge, or setback shows up in your life.

The Lover

This is all the love you have in you. When we share and radiate love around us, the world will feel it and the universe will send it back to us.

This is why you need to have an extreme amount of love inside by loving yourself, so that you find what to give. Otherwise, you will be eating up your insides and finding yourself pleasing others continuously in order to get some recognition to fill your cup. Love isn't about trade. It isn't a commercial commodity. Love is what you fill yourself with first and then you surround yourself with people who deserve you and love you.

Your primary role is to fill it up by truly loving yourself first and forgiving yourself for any past mistakes. Let go of them. Once you fill your cup with love, you will be ready to give. Because giving is living!

When you tap into the Lover inside of you, you can make every relationship flourish. You can heal a relationship that is important to you only by tapping into the Lover part of you. If you are too much in your mind and in your thoughts, couples can never find their way back. This happens when you see someone suffering or having trouble, and the first thing you want to say is, "I told you so." Because you want to ascertain you're right. So, right takes over and overrides anything else that could be there to save. If you want to save it, it comes from a place of love.

The Lover is about letting the emotional force guide you. Because when the thoughts and feelings are aligned, you will find compassion and an understanding inside of you that these are always superior to any resentment or bitterness.

If you have those negative feelings, get rid of them and replace them with positive ones. Things always happen in your life to push you to grow and to become a better version of who you are. Clearing your energy makes you feel aligned, and that's your superpower. Every action will then come from a beautiful place of love, joy, and empathy. The stronger you get in terms of your emotional intelligence, the more you will remain aligned and grounded regardless of external circumstances.

Thus, love is your inner world. And the bridge between your inner world and the outer world is communication. This is why when communication comes from a space of love, your connections will thrive and you will create healthy relationships. When you speak to someone, whatever emotional state you are in, it will appear through communication. Go to the space of love if you want to win an argument, to negotiate for an intimate relationship. The same approach wins for conflict resolution, and most importantly leads you to a great life and great success.

Find the Lover in you whenever you feel overwhelmed. The more you strengthen your emotional intelligence, the further you collapse time in the emotional space so that you can realign yourself. You can be upset for a moment, but take a deep breath in and get realigned. Use a song to lift your spirit up. Move your body to change your physiology. Dance, journal, meditate, pray. Bring yourself back to the present and ground yourself. Recall the love you have in you. Be in that field, and then take action and do.

If you are in an argument and you feel the tension going up, take a moment, ground yourself, and share it with the person you are arguing with. Don't ghost them and leave, or escalate with anger. That is not the sign of being powerful. Being powerful is remaining calm no matter what. And if you feel that the emotions are overwhelming, leave the discussion, saying, "I feel that my emotions are overwhelming, so I need to ground myself. I would like to continue the discussion in order to have powerful communication."

Sharing the truth makes you powerful and shows that you care and you are respectful. Being vulnerable makes you more powerful than any person would expect to be.

For every woman, when you communicate from an energy of love, you tap into your feminine energy. That feminine energy will help you thrive more than putting other women down or letting jealousy and envy take over your emotional space. Come back to love. Fill your heart with love, faith, and joy. This is how you trigger the Lover in you, and you nurture your relationships and all your connections. When you are filled with love and you connect to your clients or partners, they feel it. Hence, stand for the love you want to receive and you will receive it.

The Sovereign

The environment where you are is everything. A lot of becoming in life and creating is about the experience of doing it. And honoring the Sovereign in you is about creating the space for it. The Sovereign is the queen or the king, and knows that everything is going to be perfect. It commands respect from everyone, including herself. The Sovereign is the celebration of who you are.

That personality needs to have the space to feel the vibes and feel honored by her environment and all the actions she undertakes and attracts in her life. A space that's elegant, cozy, and honors your personality and what you stand for. A place where you can go and feel that you can organize things the way you want them to be.

This personality is about honoring yourself, celebrating who you are and what you have accomplished. The Sovereign in you wants to be treated with respect. That space of respect is also the space from which you communicate with others. From one Sovereign to another. This attitude will help you communicate with respect to your clients, partners, family members, and friends. It also helps you feel and be respected. We need to tap into this personality more and more.

I see that a lot in my clients in the Empowered Leaders Mastermind. One of the major transformations that happen is being able to shift into a person who receives respect from her husband, her family, or her children. Women in some parts of the world get used to being mistreated by their husbands and lacking respect in the home. They get so used to that, that feeling scared about what to expect and the mood of their husband when he gets home becomes their normal emotional home.

For example, one client in particular, who I will call Dounia. Her husband was never happy about the food she prepared, and was always complaining about the home being untidy, or his clothes never ready. The problem was that she allowed herself to be treated that way. The roots of it came from her childhood and the way she was treated growing up. Her attitude needed to change, and we started reprogramming her subconscious mind by repeating the following mantra: "I am happy and grateful that I attract respect and appreciation." Or: "I am happy and grateful that everyone respects me and appreciates what I do."

The more Dounia became familiar with these mantras, repeating them continuously, the more she started believing in her worth and that she deserved respect and appreciation. It became her vibe and it changed everything. When she heard her husband coming into the house, she changed her thinking from, *What is he going to say again? What will he complain about?* To, *I am respected by my husband and everyone.* That vibe became her new emotional home. Because the radiation of the vibe precedes any action and any communication coupled with discipline, magic happened. After more than two and a half months, one day her husband told her how much he appreciated what she was doing in the house and in her work. Becoming your own queen brings incredible vibes into your life.

It takes discipline, perseverance, and on-going awareness about your thoughts and the blockage you create in your mind. When you feel down despite all of the goodwill and following the process, it's okay. It happens to all of us, even to me. I will put on music to lift my spirits. I'm a fan of Jennifer Lopez and her continuous growth and re-creation. Move, dance, journal, remember your goals. Sit in front of your work, adjust your crown on your head, and be the queen.

That is the space from which you lead yourself to success and to wealth creation. This is also the space from which you communicate from a Sovereign to a Sovereign. Whether it's for a new job, a new recruit, to sell a product or a service, or to show up as a leader in your field of expertise. Make your actions and all your doing under the theme of Sovereign to Sovereign. You will create a brand of respect and alignment with your favorite style and way of being. It can be luxury, polished and sophisticated, or more raw, natural, and wild. Whichever you choose, be in alignment with who you are inside of you when you feel safe to let it be expressed as it comes from a space of love and respect to yourself and to others.

Open your awareness of the things that you're thinking about and feeling. For example, look at the places where you are selling yourself short, by underpricing your offer or being underpaid. What are the places where you feel that you are not deserving to be where you are, and you have that daunting feeling that something is missing or not right? Don't take it as a sign, it simply means that you have a voice inside of your head that isn't cheering you up, but rather discouraging you. Ask yourself, where am I not fully aligned? What is that place inside that's still holding me down? Check behind the curtain, look for who you are when no one is watching and open the door to your Sovereign to come out and to hold the space for you. Get aligned with it at the three levels: your thoughts, your feelings, and your actions. Grow and let the Sovereign flourish as you move in alignment with it at those three levels of being. Create a space in your house where you celebrate that Sovereign in you, use it as a reference—pillows, candles, flowers, silk, harmonious colors—so that you connect your brain with the place. Then make it in every room of your house and everywhere you go.

The Sovereign in you will attract more of the circumstances to reconfirm your sovereignty and the emotional state of mind around that personality. We become what we think of, what we experience at the emotional level. Choose to be aligned with the Sovereign in you. Everything will change around you to make it truly happen. Because "I am my power" and "You are your power." The emotional power in you makes you who you are.

Leadership is in the space of sovereignty because being a leader isn't about telling people what to do, it's about inspiring people to follow you and to choose to be guided by your leadership. This is why this personality is about leading yourself first so that you can lead others with that same energy. In particular for the female world, women are human beings that sync up to each other. When two women communicate, they look each other in the eyes and then sync into the created emotions about a story, news, or whatever they're sharing. Women calibrate their energy continuously. This is why the Masterminds have such a powerful impact, as they create a collective intelligence and make it possible to exponentially multiply the created energy around success, money, wealth, joy, happiness, health, and relationships. It is essential to choose who you're surrounding yourself with, because you become the average of the handful of people you spend most of the time with.

Happiness, success, and celebrations are contagious. The more it is expressed and shared, the more women calibrate to that level of vibes and it will start impacting their lives. This is how we have created a community of thousands of female leaders from all around the world to inspire each other, motivate each other, and respect and love each other.

Use respect, love, and kindness and keep your boundaries clear. You're not to compromise the respect for yourself by anybody, starting with yourself. Honor yourself every day. Honor the Sovereign in you no matter what.

---

1. www.balmethod.com

My Workbook - Chapter 4

What part of my life needs more of the Magician in it?

What will I create as the most powerful Warrior?

Who will I call today to say, "I love you?"

What is my new routine to honor the Sovereign in me?

5

The Codes of Self-Leadership

Becoming a leader isn't a role that is given to you, it's a role you take. It isn't a job that you apply for, it's a job you embody. A responsibility you decide willingly to have and to embody. It comes naturally when it aligns with the service you provide, and the voice you carry to help others, to drive the world towards a better future.

All leaders have one thing and only one thing in common and that is the followers. Being a leader has nothing to do with the rank, the seniority, or the credentials—it is about the capacity to inspire followers who volunteer to follow you. The way you can attract followers. It was either by manipulating people or by inspiring them.

Manipulating people happens through manipulative marketing, innovation, fear, or aspirational images. But none of the manipulation breeds loyalty and trust. All it does is cause more stress and tension.

The only way to stand out and to find followers is inspiration, which comes from sharing the story behind why the leader is the one to stand out. The why behind the work you do. You need to have clarity around the why so that your community of followers will emotionally connect with what you were able to articulate for them. Besides the why, you need to have the discipline around what you do and how you do it. And you need to be consistent in everything you do, making it a reflection of what you truly believe.

Leadership is about the capacity to communicate effectively and to put our desire and our beliefs into words. The great leader helps put into words who we are and what we feel. This is why leadership is creating trust and loyalty.

As social animals, we crave the human experience of trust and belonging. Thus, finding a leader that articulates eloquently what we believe and our deepest values is a gift. It makes us feel drawn because we recognize those feelings. They feel home. They give a sense of true belonging and being part of a community. Those feelings are so powerful. They turn the leader into a magnet to everything around.

Every Woman Is Born a Leader

Every woman is born with the potential to realize the highest role she wishes to access. She can be a president, an entrepreneur, a leader ... so much to aspire to.

Today, women increasingly have options. They can choose to embark on diverse careers and advance as far as their innate capacity and hard work will carry them. Women can attain leadership and decision-making positions, not just by piling up advanced degrees, but also by launching successful ventures and innovative products.

So, what holds women back?

The environment a girl grows up in can largely influence how she shows up in the world. If she is told, "Girls can't do that!" she will have a difficult time realizing her innate potential to contribute to the health and vitality of the workplace. All of this can keep her small, lacking confidence, and drowning in frustration.

What do women need to get themselves out of this vicious cycle? They need role models to inspire them, and the skills to power up and raise their confidence. They need a support system that ignites their passion for service and for leading. Women need to feel safe, and safe to create a nurturing environment for others.

This was my drive when I created the Believe-Act-Lead Method. For every woman to be able to *be* in the emotional state of what she wants to see and attract in her life. When you believe in yourself and in the possibilities, you become that new identity and you are able to *be* the person you are striving to create, the goal achieved by you. The taking actions and the doing will not matter if you don't have that emotional force. You will be repeating the same patterns and the same results over and over again. Only then, when you combine the two—your emotional strength with a well-structured strategy for actions and doing—will you become unstoppable. The level of wealth and success you will attract to you are incredible.

This is what the Believe-Act-Lead Method is about. It gives women the tools, techniques, and discipline to turn their life around. It installs the Warrior in you when you need it. It makes the Magician your normal way of tackling life, and creating magic and infinite possibilities. It honors the Sovereign in you and brings all the respect, and it will celebrate with the love and gratitude continuous wins and incredible achievements.

Sandra was already a Managing Director when she started the Mastermind. The main focus was to improve her self-confidence and her attitude. Because, despite her responsibility, she was feeling like a little girl when she was in a meeting with her president. Despite her good performance and her work, Sandra was still nervous each time she had those leadership meetings. The Sovereign in her was not consistent and we focused on bringing it and owning it. It started by creating that space in her own house and celebrating the amazing person she is where no one is watching. Before we even finished the three months, she was nominated a member of the board of a financial institution. Her change of attitude brought her more recognition to help her grow and own her space because she deserves the place where she is.

Yes, of course you can turn your life around! That's when you take all your personalities into effective action to design your dream life, to connect the dots and to achieve your money goals!

To do that you need to lead yourself. No one will if it doesn't come from you. Empowerment is about unlocking the codes of self-leadership so that you can lead yourself to your goals, your dreams, and your most impossible objectives.

Lead With An Empowering Energy

The previous chapters were about the emotional force and raising the vibrations up. But it showed that everyone—every woman, man, human being—has the potential to realize the highest role wished to be accessed. Leading with your vibes means to lead a life that vibes forward. Because your vibes speak before you do. Your vibes walk into the room before you do. Maya Angelou once said about her confidence and her gratitude going up on stage, when she walks, she takes every positive person in her life with her. Those emotions precede her and make her shine.

That is what you do, let your positive emotions and high vibration lead you. Use joy, happiness, and kindness to lead yourself. People around you are calibrating to your vibes and you will attract people looking to calibrate to those vibes.

To become that leader will not happen overnight. It isn't about one action that you will do, or one thing that you do.

In his leadership work, Simon Sinek demonstrated it starting from the question of, "When did you know that you love your wife or your husband?" The love in a relationship is not about the events or the intensity, it's about the consistency. It is about the caring that you show every day to your partner. Same with going to the gym. Going for one whole day will not get you into shape. It's exercising for twenty minutes every day that will get you the results you want.

The same thing about being a leader. It isn't about going to an intensive seminar for a weekend or a week and getting a certificate that will make you a leader. No, it's the boring repetition of actions and the way of being that will get you into becoming the incredible leader you are destined to be.

You don't fall in love with your partner because he brings you flowers or takes you to a nice restaurant. You fall in love with your partner when he wakes up in the morning and says good morning before he looks at his phone. When he gets himself a glass of water and gets one for you as well. When you are hurt and have gone through a painful day, he doesn't start sharing all his successes and achievements, or tell you, "I told you so," to prove that he is always right. She fell in love with you because when she was tired that day, you left the room quiet to give her the space to be.

It is the succession and cumulation of those actions that lead you to wake up one day and say, "I love him." Leadership is the same thing. It's not what you say one day, that will cause people to say you are a leader and want to follow you. It's the culmination of many actions and things that wouldn't matter if they are done by themselves that will make you a leader.

When you do things consistently and you show up as a leader every day. When you connect with people and ask about them because you truly care. It's what you do every day that will make people want to work with you, want to be with you, and will love being around you. It comes down to bringing that sisterhood and brotherhood out of strangers. To be able to create the relationship of sisters and brothers, you need to commonly believe in the same values.

Choose the Vibes of Gratitude and Love

Traveling with four children during the summer time after the world opened up following COVID was a moment for me to appreciate how my mindset had shifted. It was incredible where I was able to prove hands-on all the concepts I teach and stand for, applying them to every step in your life and to every part of the day.

We experienced a missed flight, a delayed flight, a missed connection, and a change in the itinerary. Traveling with my four children, these events could have been very annoying. But this time, it was different. I was filled with gratitude for every moment. Every extra hour of a flight delay, the change of the routing or the program, I was thankful. I enjoyed writing and preparing a new incredible program for leadership and wealth creation, and talking with my boy and the girls. I was discovering with them what we see and whom we meet on our way.

I found myself on an unexpected trip to New York with the children. Walking on Fifth Avenue. Standing in front of Rockefeller Center and feeling the intensity of Times Square. The lights, the music, the fun, the celebrations. Enjoying every step, holding hands with my children.

This moment took me back to the summer of 1994 when my father took us to New York for the first time: me and my two sisters. His gift to us before connecting to Boston as I was starting my graduate studies at Harvard University.

We were mesmerized and speechless. We were overly excited, like little girls in a candy store. We were so impressed by the skyscrapers, the Statue of Liberty. I was amazed by the people in the streets. Women in suits and walking in sports shoes before changing into heels for the office.

It felt like stepping into the movies we dreamed about for so long. Movies we watched over and over on video cassettes. We were inside of the TV series *I'll Take Manhattan*. Although, at that time we could never figure out what the title meant. Until we walked into Manhattan.

The incredible streets and the infinite avenues. The hot dog stands, the ice cream trucks ... all the colors of New York. That was the day I knew what it meant opening the gate to a new world! New possibilities! It truly felt like a magical dream. And that is how you should live your life on a daily basis, embracing every moment and celebrating the beauty of life. I developed such a deep appreciation of discovering new places, new cultures, and the way people live their lives.

During that time, my sisters and I were grateful for every moment. Any change, any setback, was an experience. We were so happy with the few words of English we had learned to sing Madonna, George Michael, and Whitney Houston songs.

I embraced every part of it, and I was grateful for every second. Truly connected with my inner strength and light. Incredibly young and naïve.

I knew so deeply that there was energy bigger than us, the infinite intelligence, the divine light, and the cosmic perfection that guided us.

That infinite intelligence, the divine power took me to New York, and to Harvard University. And also to meeting high leaders and heads of state, and being part of incredible global events. I can still feel the thrill of being part of high-level decision-making and contributing to the development and to a world free of poverty. I embrace every part of that mission. Everything in it. Traveling around the world, discovering the most remote places working on World Bank projects and initiatives, from Hanoi in Vietnam to Vientiane in Laos, to Manilla in the Philippines, to Jaipur in India, Trinidad, and Tobago, to Buenos Aires in Argentina, to Prague for the World Bank Annual meetings. I spent time in places all around the world that shaped my love for impact and development. These places anchored my appreciation for cultural differences and traditions. I was part of incredible projects and global initiatives and worked in the most distinguished offices.

There is a light completely aligned with the vibration of gratitude and the vibration of love for yourself and others. This is the vibration of a heart-centered mission for the development of the world. Today, this vibration is about wanting good and empowerment for every woman. It's the vibration of believing and trusting the universe and the divine.

Life is a gift, and everything happens for you not against you. We get the best out of it when we are grateful for every moment we experience. It starts to happen when you embrace the duality of what comes your way.

It begins unfolding when you surrender and trust. You will start profoundly believing.

Finally, your journey is yours to make. Use gratitude to make it and celebrate every moment.

Every day, feel the joy of an amazing moment in your life and lead your way with the vibes of gratitude and love.

Success and Wealth Are All Yours

For every woman and man I encounter as part of the BAL Method Mastermind, comes knowing that the big wealth and success they desire and deserve are on their way, but they haven't seen the evidence of it ... yet.

I went from being an inhibited young woman growing up in Morocco, where I was expected to marry young and settle down, to becoming a millionaire entrepreneur and among Forbes's "100 Most Powerful Women in the World" *while* raising four beautiful children with the man I desired to partner with in life.

In hindsight, I know this all happened because I had uncovered and embodied the codes of self-leadership to wealth.

As I continue to embody these codes, I have also become a catalyst for the professional woman and female entrepreneur who is ready to unleash her self-leadership, create her desired wealth, impact through her heart and service, and shine her authentic light of truth into the world.

As I'm going through my own leveling up, my understanding is deepening of the connection between the divine power of infinite intelligence and the phenomenal energy inside each one of us.

Client activation has accordingly leveled up, and their tangible results are off the charts. Donna, for example, was able to sign a 100K contract immediately after she restructured her business and repurposed her branding. When she changed her emotional state, she was able to approach things differently.

Imen, who moved back to Tunisia when the pandemic hit and consequently left her great career as an international environmental consultant, was able to articulate her dream that she left silent inside of her. She became a TV star in Tunisia, being part of two programs about women's empowerment. Similar results for Canada-based Bouchra, through her podcast, who's become a voice for every woman who has had to leave her country and recreate herself in the West. All while raising her family with tradition and modernity.

What Does Leadership Mean?

Leadership is not about gaining authority and power. It is about being able to show up in a way that also empowers your peers, your community, your clients, your team, and your family to grow with you.

When you embody that understanding of leadership truly and profoundly, it becomes a mission on its own. It represents the reason why you want to show up and share value from a space of service, of helping and giving. With emotional energy of caring, loving, and connecting.

And this applies to everything you do, from your work to your service, your consulting expertise to your managerial responsibilities. The same thing will affect and shape your family, relationships, and friends.

For business in particular, this will not only change the way you perceive business but how you articulate your business model, and how you take on your day.

It will help you show up authentically and be genuine. Connecting truly and caring by giving space for others.

By shifting my way of being and the way I connect with everyone—starting from showing up consistently and caring about others, to sharing values because I deeply want women to know that they can succeed and create the life that they dream about—it's incredible the level of connections I created within the journey of the BAL Method. Not to mention the number of followers attracted to the concept, the model, and what it stands for, which is empowered female leaders who are leading themselves by creating wealth and making an impact. **My drive is to help every woman be her natural best and find her guiding mechanism inside of her to create joy, success, happiness, and fulfillment.** Each one evaluates success depending on her environment, her understanding, and how she grows up.

Leadership Is About Adapting to Change

Traveling with my four children calls for great adaptation. It's a sports competition, with detailed attention. Time has a different meaning.

There's no sense in rushing when they don't feel like rushing. No reason to choose the meal, the shirt, or the shoe for them ... they will do whatever they feel like anyway. No need to look at the watch, they have their own system.

And when the ages vary from five to ten, thirteen to fifteen, you need to adapt four times differently. The more I deepen my work on mindset and energetics, the more I find myself grounded, peaceful, and grateful around them, no matter how overly excited or stimulated they are.

If we take one hour to do something that could be done in five minutes, I take it as a trip on its own. If we eat four days of noodles in a row because my five year old said so, it's an experience. If we decide to go swim again after we have finished showering, it is the second part of the day. And all is okay.

Each one of us has his or her own pace. Each one of us has his or her own preference. The business works exactly the same way as any of those relationships. Besides the importance of resilience and caring, it requires innovation, creativity, agility, and of course adaptability.

And everything in life follows the same concept. That's exactly what the famous quote, often incorrectly connected to Charles Darwin states: "It is not the strongest of the species that survives, nor the most intelligent that survives. It is the one that is the most adaptable to change. In the struggle for survival, the fittest win out at the expense of their rivals because they succeed in adapting themselves best to their environment."

So business, my friends, is about survival within an increasingly competitive environment. It's about finding your uniqueness, leading through it, adapting to that very environment, and offering great value through your work and your presence. When you focus on the service, the help you provide, and the value you offer, you can start to create your own circumstances so that you can reach your goal no matter what.

The digital era and the rise of artificial intelligence are making change inevitable in every area of our life. This is why adaptability should become your competitive advantage in anything you do. That is your cutting-edge skill.

You will get all the requirements to be an athlete in your business and in your life. Gather all your adaptability gears and inner power to be the winner in this ever-changing environment and to lead yourself through a great life.

The Codes of Self-Leadership

In general, becoming a leader is about knowing how to lead others. It's also seen as being a reference and a light in your industry and in your domain of expertise.

It is true that being a leader starts by leading yourself first to the excellence you're seeking and by making your mission a reality.

Nevertheless, leading yourself is not only about being an expert in your field and mastering every facet of it. In other words, it isn't just about spending the ten thousand hours to confirm yourself as an expert and as a reference. Expertise and knowledge are essential but they're not enough.

What makes a difference between leaders, experts, and successful people is the ability to lead themselves through their emotional states and through the struggles and challenges which come their way.

When you hold on to your mission and to a bigger vision, you start embodying some of the codes of self-leadership to thrive no matter what, to succeed no matter what, and pave the way for others through your leadership journey.

This is why to be able to lead yourself, it is essential to embody all the codes of self-leadership, and to use your genius and your uniqueness to guide yourself.

The First Three Codes

Once you understand that designing your life is your responsibility, you will shift into a new level of energetics and possibilities. Although it seems easy at first, that transition may take deeper work, discipline, and the will to be in charge and create a new life.

The first three Codes of Self-leadership will put you on a track to brilliance, success, and infinite possibilities. And I am writing a whole book that will be dedicated to sharing the twelve codes of self-leadership I have compiled to transform your life by unleashing the power in you and becoming a true leader in your field and in the world.

Code 1: Making the unshakable decision to change fast. Becoming in charge of your life and designing what you truly want to have in your life is the first step to reaching success. We grow up having our decisions made for us through our parents, and we get used to that. And then, we are faced with a reality where we need to learn how to make sound decisions and stick to them.

In fact, successful people make decisions very fast and change them slowly. While people who have difficulties in life make decisions very slowly, and then they change them fast and often. When you make a decision to improve to lead yourself, you flip your brain and your thinking. Thus, you start operating at a different level that will get you closer to your goal.

Code 2: Changing the old, limiting beliefs that are stopping you is the start of your self-leadership. In other words, creating new beliefs to help you reach your goals and make your dreams a reality. When you focus on your mission and a big goal you set up for yourself, make it your focus, and don't let any old thinking or discouragement move you away from that goal. You need to become your own cheerleader, your own stimulation, and your own motivation. That is what it means to be a leader of yourself!

Code 3: Integrate one productive action in your daily programming. One productive habit will get you closer to your goal. You will instill that discipline by repeating the productive habit. The secret to reaching success in what you do is to integrate discipline into your life. Discipline helps you transform productive actions into daily habits. When you can understand the importance of habit in shaping your life, you will be ready to let go of habits that are not serving you and not helping to get closer to your objectives.

Lead Yourself to Success

By embodying these first three codes of self-leadership you will be able to start noticing changes in your life through a mood and emotional shift. When you can shift emotionally, that translates into vibrations and frequencies. These frequencies are the energetics that help us attract what we want to see happening in our lives.

This is why we focus a lot on the mindset in the first phase of our Empowered Leaders Mastermind. When you work on your mindset, you will automatically improve your productivity and your creativity. Which is why taking a moment to assess the emotional state we are in and understanding the thoughts and beliefs holding us back are essential. That's exactly what makes a difference between great success and a continuous journey of trying to be.

Success is not about doing different things. It's about doing things differently. And that differently is about the emotional state.

My Workbook - Chapter 5

What is the unshakable decision I am making today?

What is an old habit that is not helping today?

How will I change that old habit and what will I replace it with?

One productive action I am taking today:

6

Access Financial Intelligence

My story with money has taken different colors through the years. I worked with high level money, so millions and billions of dollars were financial flows that made my daily work. So while my money paradigm did not have my own money in it, it was creating the level of impact. Working in development, money is never about us. It's always about others, about how big the project is, how big the program is, and how big the impact is. Therefore, the bigger it is, the more work there is to be done. I was trained this way.

Then I started to deepen my understanding about the readiness for money overflow for oneself, and how to attract money in your life so that you can reach your own money freedom and not only be good at structuring money for others. Because the paradigm is different. There is that feeling of "it is not for me" that grows into a money blockage for oneself.

If you really want time and money freedom, you have to be willing and able to change your paradigm with money. Otherwise, you will be getting the same results you have been experiencing all these years.

Money is the energy currency that represents our energy at work. This energy works when you are selling, buying, creating, and simply being. Money flows in and out, reflecting the energy around you.

This chapter is about financial intelligence, by mastering your needs when it comes to money, and feeling autonomous. This is particularly important for money because money freedom brings a sense of worthiness and being valued.

This chapter is at the heart of the money paradigm and your relationship with money. It will also give you clarity regarding your definition of your financial needs, how you can use it as an objective, and reverse engineer from it to articulate a strategy and an action plan to reach it.

The Money Paradigm

We grow up hearing how money has to be earned by working hard, by studying hard. I had an uncle who was always complaining about the unfairness of money distribution. He insisted on spreading to all of us, very young at that time, how you need money to make money, so it was hopeless from the start. But I had his own brother thinking differently, always saying that the most beautiful flower could blossom out of a pile of trash ... which balanced my hopes up. Nevertheless, there are many tags attached to the way we perceive money and the way we relate to it. All these tags are related to the misconception and the way we are programmed to think of money. Just the thought of it, or the sight, will trigger all these old habits of hearing about it and thinking about it.

It can be related to fear of lacking it and not having access to it when you need it. It can also be linked to growing up hearing that you need to work hard to earn money. Or being around people who are juggling several jobs and several projects to make ends meet. Money is also linked to being a bad person as several stories on TV and in movies show a negative image of people with a lot of money. Likewise, it can be considered dirty and make you feel that it's better to have barely enough of it to feel content. In addition, money is linked to complications, so people go through their life without trying to make more money because it is connected with the potential problems that it could bring along. This is why money brings so many conflicts, confusion, and bitterness with it.

All of these thoughts and arguments shape the way we think about money and the way we connect the thoughts around it. Changing the habitual way of thinking and emotionally connecting with money requires a whole process of healing and paradigm shift. Trends in the way societies approach money can take many years to change. Like the ATM ... it took twenty-five years before they became completely familiar to everyone. People preferred to go to the banks and get their money from a teller instead of using their cards and the machine. They didn't trust the whole technology. And stories about stolen cards and stolen numbers were present in everyone's minds, blocking people from trusting the ATMs.

We don't need the change towards the money to take that many years, because when you work with the underlying paradigm, you can create a profound mindset shift. We put ourselves in a box in terms of the limitation of the money we can earn, or what we can consider possible. And societies, news, stories, families, toxicities corrupt further the voice inside of our head, making the box feel tighter. These blockages become the reality we see. Because when we analyze what we are aligned with, it will be all those limiting paradigms.

The money paradigm needs to shift and the energy of money has to be aligned with everything outside of that very box. Unfortunately, we can only be aligned with the thoughts we have in our head, and these thoughts have been programmed for many years. So the mindset shift can come only when you make the unshakable decision to do so.

As an example, when you think about the difficulties of attracting money and being worried about not finishing up the month, you can attract only that at the end for yourself. So, your alignment is with the worries and the energy of scarcity. The money flow gets blocked by your self-doubt and your continuous repetition of discouraging thoughts.

Abundance works differently. It starts from a different set of thoughts and feelings. Abundance requires continuous awareness of the thoughts that come to your mind. There is a sequence to be designed and followed to get yourself aligned with the abundance of wealth and the energy of money. It starts with defining goals and objectives that are so broad that it will be hard for you to dismiss them.

Create new patterns for yourself so that you don't get into a destructive, repetitive thought sequence. So that your only way out is you rise. The more you try to understand what is happening to you, the more you will be creating the same patterns that you have made a home for yourself. The feeling that things wouldn't work anyway or you thought so anyway. Let go of this habitual way of approaching anything. Zoom out from your habitual pattern by creating something new and different. Be consistent with it so that you rise to another level. Use stimulation through beautiful music, water, waves, and meditation sound.

Make Your Objectives So Big ... It Will Be Hard to Dismiss Them

Broadening your perspectives helps you keep the focus and not sabotage yourself when you see that you're not achieving small objectives with the tight deadlines you gave yourself.

We set goals to stay focused. We set goals to know where we are going.

However, you should never let those goals become an emotional triggering factor when you don't see that goal becoming a reality, and you get yourself into a spiral of frustration and unworthiness. Because that makes your goals limited and easy to dismiss. This way of thinking will put too much pressure on making money.

Because making money becomes an end on its own, and it will start feeling so far away and difficult to reach that it will guide your thoughts to a negative spiral. That is what will stimulate you in the wrong direction and will tamper your relationship with money. Instead, embrace it through your readiness to welcome limitless wealth, limitless impact, incredible relationship, and abundance. This should feel like your openness to attract incredible wealth in your lifetime. It isn't about the exact number because you cannot know the amount, or rather limit the amount of what you can receive and manifest. You can get ready to celebrate every milestone and step that will get you closer to your objectives in terms of money creation.

You can approach these new levels of frequency by consciously becoming an energetic match for celebrations around wealth and every positive thing you attract in your life. You start feeling ready to connect with the beauty of wealth and the wins you can have in your life. That's the secret of staying strong around your beliefs. Because alignment is exceedingly fragile. It can be very sensitive because our brain and our thoughts are constantly looking for something to align to. And your only job is to make sure that your awareness is always positive and clean. Thoughts can change in a fraction of a millisecond all the time, and the easiest thing to align to is what you are believing in.

The most important thing for you is to stay in alignment with these thoughts and not dismiss them because you find the perfectly logical explanation for how you cannot create them. When you truly embrace that if you succeed or fail with money, you will use the experience to draw the lessons and your understanding about how to calibrate to making wealth and creating money faster. These lessons will not only help you grow and advance, but will be good for everyone around you.

If you feel that you shouldn't be focusing on money because all you want to do is help others, and create a better life for your children, your family, and others, you're actually creating a blockage differently. Wealth creation isn't about greed and wanting to collect money just to collect money. Wealth creation is creating choices in your life and possibilities for more impact. This is why it is time to shift the way you relate to wealth creation by linking it to the possibility of what you can create around you and how much impact you can have.

One thing for certain, is that when you're creating wealth and making money, you are showing others what's possible. This is why if I succeed or I fail in making the money I am planning to receive at the end of the month, I will always draw the lessons from it so that I can calibrate to wealth faster for me and to share it with you. This way, my work and all the efforts I extend are not only for me, but also for you and us.

When I start looking at how every difficulty on the way to creating wealth for me is also for others, it brings me back to my broader context: I have embarked on my mission to help women grow confident, resilient, tech-savvy, and financially free. The financial part takes a deep understanding of numbers, strategy, and energetics.

It helps me protect my belief system from rejecting those thoughts about the goals and objectives. This is the only way to stay aligned with your thoughts around money. Otherwise, you will always find something super logical and structured to prove to you that it's impossible to think that you can attract more money than what society thought you should receive with your level of diplomas and studies, and depending on your gender or where you live.

When your goal is bigger, failure, setback, or a month with no results will not stop you from continuing your path to reach it. Because the picture in your mind is larger. The context is broader, and the horizon is therefore long term.

When you keep your objectives aligned with a big vision and a broad context, it helps you create a large, safe bubble where you let your creativity grow and make it feel that it's your stage even when no one is watching.

When your context is broad, your journey will hold many stories. All the ups and downs will help you build resilience. And your context will make the road worth every part of it.

To get to that level, you need to ensure that every fiber and every thought, even the small thoughts, should be aligned with what you want to create. This is how you can build your vibration from true alignment.

Once your mission is aligned with who you really are and with all your beliefs, it will trigger all the power from your inside. Fear will be surpassed by your inner drive to turn your big vision into reality. Finally, when you keep your goals and objectives broad, they become your legacy.

This way you will stop getting into a self-sabotaging mood as soon as something doesn't go your way. Instead, you will learn with time how to zoom out from difficulties by looking at the larger picture. And this is how you transform your life by believing in your mission, acting on it with a clear, strategic plan, and leading yourself to greatness.

The Law of Compensation is About Money

To create the money that you want, you need to master your numbers and how much you want to make. Of course, this isn't enough except that it will require you to align your belief about receiving that amount of money so that you can hold it in your hand.

Through the years, I have learned that money is an exchange for the value you provide. Master the value you provide and make sure that it's excellent and the best you have. Find out what your great gift is, what service and offer you provide, and whom you're serving. At that moment the only thing you have to focus on is providing the best value.

The Law of Compensation states that the money you receive is correlated with three things. The first is the need for what you do in terms of the service you provide or the product you offer. The second is your ability to do what you are doing. In other words, it is about the excellence of your expertise and your service. And the third is the difficulty there will be in replacing you.

Applying the Law of Compensation and understanding what each component encompasses is how you can feel in harmony with the universe. Therefore, for you to increase the wealth you would attract in your life, it is essential to focus on becoming the best and the greatest in what you do.

So focus on providing the best value, and give it your all. Show up and be present even if you think that nobody is watching. Grow your expertise and your knowledge about your industry so that you become the go-to expert and you shine through your mastering of the service and the product you provide. Keep all your energy on making yourself the best in what you do and creating a mindset of abundance. Open your arms to truly express and celebrate your readiness to receive the wealth and the money that is yours.

I became an entrepreneur in 2014 when my boy turned seven years old and I had two little girls of four and almost two years old. I was very busy as a mother and I wanted to be able to have flexibility and freedom at the same time. I trusted my dedication to making entrepreneurship work and to create a reference in sustainability, strategic growth, and impact finance. It was the start of my journey as a strategic consultant and an impact investment specialist. I believed so strongly and deeply in my mission, and I was confident in my expertise, continuing every day to grow in terms of knowledge and experience. I embodied the real meaning of continuing evolution and growth. I knew about my niche, my offer, and my value. All that marketing gurus were insisting on without even knowing I was doing that. I was following my intuition and my intuition was strong and loud. Deep inside of me, I knew the importance of helping institutions and organizations set up a portfolio of projects to help them become greener and aligned with sustainable development goals. I reached seven figures in the second year and I was growing, building trust, and becoming a reference in sustainable development, renewable energies, and resource optimization for a better future. Then I reached eight figures while I was working, all the time surrounded by my children.

However, something that was missing in this puzzle was my relationship with money creation. So I was continuously worried that something wouldn't work well. It pushed me to be in a pleasing mood so that I could feel the comforting voice of praise and recognition.

Suddenly, I was faced with one of the biggest challenges I was fearing so much. This was the nightmare of any entrepreneur, but by fearing, I had attracted it into my life. Money was lost and I found myself deep in bitterness, sadness, and self-deprecation.

I had two choices at that moment. My first choice was to stay in the rabbit hole, feel sorry, and honor that situation but reassure myself that I knew that entrepreneurship was a risky business when you connect with people you don't know and you don't trust. The second choice was to live through this very hard moment and survive so that the fear of it happening and the fear of failure as an entrepreneur had no power or control over me anymore.

When you harmonize with your surroundings and all types of experiences you go through, you discover there is beauty in that moment of sadness and pain. It pushes you to connect with the joy and gratitude for what is available. There's a reason I had to go through all of what I have gone through. It transformed me to become the person I am today. It pushed me to understand more about the energetics of how to succeed and keep things alive. Understanding the energy around what you experience and what you attract in your life. Harmonizing is like finding the colors of the rainbow when it's raining and suddenly the bright sun pops out from behind the clouds. The beauty of the colors illustrates the feeling of that harmony.

The manifestation sequence applies in two directions. In manifesting big money and big wealth, and in manifesting what we fear by getting aligned with it. Thinking about every possible consequence, and when something happens you confirm to yourself how you have been right all the way. It feels like you are honoring the sadness and the problem by getting ready to receive it. The same reasoning goes around self-deprecation when people prefer to hurt themselves and treat themselves badly so that if someone does it, they will be prepared anyway. It usually comes from experience or hearing the voice of someone who hurt you in the past and you couldn't let go of it. It can also be coming from a space of manipulation so that people will praise you and show you that they care.

When you honor your life with the good and the hard part of it, you will grow in terms of conscious awareness and maturity. Every part matters. You can attract incredible things in your life when you embrace and celebrate every small part. Because it takes little things to create amazing things in your life.

This is why making money is not about money. In his book, *It's Not About Money*, Bob Proctor explains how many people live a lie. That lie keeps them average their whole life. People who live an average life convince themselves that they aren't special enough to live a life of wealth. People keep on repeating that to themselves until they start believing that they cannot do otherwise. This way, being average is the worst of the best and the best of the worst.

Changing your money paradigm is your choice. No one will make that decision for you, or will oblige you to do so.

There are two secrets of making money and they both are counter-intuitive. Because making money is not about money. **The first secret is that when you want to be making money, you do not focus on that**. You focus on giving all the benefits and the value to your clients, in whatever industry. Focusing on making the clients feel that all that matters to you is their well-being. The simplest illustration is a retail store having a sale. Buyers flock to the store because they think that the store owner isn't after their wallets but interested in delivering real benefits for people.

The second secret to making money is not to miss the opportunity to do so. That opportunity only comes after you've built rapport with your potential clients by genuinely and humbly serving them. They trust you because you've been honest and helpful from the start. You're a genuine human being, interested in helping other human beings obtain what they want.

Three Money Strategies

There are three different money strategies you can choose depending on what you're looking for in terms of wealth creation, as well as the level of time and money freedom you're looking for.

The majority of people, more than ninety-five percent, are trading time for money. Which means that the income is determined by the time spent doing the work. There will always be a limit in the money gained through this generalized model. No matter how hard you work with this strategy, whatever you can make in terms of money will always be capped. Because there are only a certain number of hours in the day—and no matter how hard you try, or how high you price your one hour of work, there will always be a limit—and you will need to work harder to grow your wealth and that's opposite to what the laws of the universe are stating about attracting wealth and abundance, this strategy is the natural one. The one school prepares us to do. Getting good grades, to be accepted in the best colleges and universities so that we can get the best job. In our normal way of thinking, the best job is a job that is stable, secure, and where you can get promoted and increase your salary with time. You will open a retirement plan and everything will seem clear and predictable.

Our brain is structured to feel safe and not have any risk of failure. That strategy is completely in line with how we have been programmed since we were children.

The second strategy covers three to four percent of the population, where money is used to generate more money. Money is invested in order to make more money. This strategy applies primarily to generational wealth, where money is already there and all it takes is to invest it and let it work for you. That will be investing in real estate, stocks, funds, and companies. Money works on itself and gets compounded through dividends.

The third strategy is one percent of the population. But this one percent of the population owns ninety-six percent of the wealth in the world. Their strategy is based on the creation of multiple sources of income, allowing them to make money in their sleep. That is the best strategy for money. It has its rules. When you're a new entrepreneur or a solopreneur, it takes putting into place one good, stable source before launching several ones at the same time.

So what is the best strategy for you?

The last one is the best strategy, and the creation of multiple sources of income can apply to you even if you are an employee. In addition to your salary, you can receive bonuses for good work, and a percentage for referral or for sales. All of these different ways to calculate an income represent different sources of income.

Master Your Magic Number

You can choose the money strategy that seems the most appropriate for you depending on how you handle the potential fear about the future and about money creation. Nevertheless, to know where you are going, you need to be able to master your numbers. Which means that instead of worrying about whether or not you will align, focus on your Magic Number and the strategic plan you have set up for yourself. When you trust that, it will all unfold as you not only master your expertise, but you stay connected to the sequence of wealth manifestation. The emotional piece will put it all together as you surrender to the universal magic and to your faith.

That is the attitude of the winner. If you were to compare this to something you eat that would be a cake. When you taste a cake, you will not feel that the eggs are good, or the flour is special. It's the whole cake together that feels perfect. All the ingredients are there in perfect harmony. It is the love you put into it while preparing, the expertise for the stirring of all the ingredients, and it finishes with the exact time for cooking, the exact temperature. All of these together make the perfect cake. Not one without the other.

This is why you can be a wiz in finance, but if the attitude is not there, if the emotional energy is off, you will be just a finance expert your whole life, helping others make money and contributing to the dream of someone else. If you want to be the star of your own movie, and not let someone else be the star while you take the second role of just the figurine, you have to master the balance in your life, the universal harmony, and hype up your emotional intelligence.

However, mastering your numbers will give you the frame for it to unfold within. Like a structure where you can watch your beautiful life unfolding with grace and elegance, just like if there was the most beautiful music in the background. This music is you feeling the harmony in your life with the cosmic power, the divine, and the events unfolding before you. Day after day, celebrating every moment, feeling grateful for your growth and your evolution over time.

To calculate your Magic Number, you will take an empty piece of paper and put down all of your necessities for a month. Everything you're required to spend so that you can feel that you have a comfortable life and that you don't need to ever worry about making ends meet. The list will include:

- Housing

- Electricity, water, gas
- Car
- Groceries
- School
- Health
- Hobbies
- Traveling
- Feeling good (spa, hairdresser, massage, treating yourself)
- Extras

= total .... X 12 = ... (A)

Once you calculate the sum of all these numbers, multiply it by twelve months, so that you can get the total for a whole year. This number will represent your needs for a year, which I will refer to as (A).

It's important to integrate what makes you feel happy and complete and not just privileging others. The exercise will help you stretch your thinking up to the number of years you want to live comfortably with the same lifestyle without ever worrying about money or the lack of it.

Studies showed people live to an average of eighty-five years old, but you can make it ninety if you prefer. From that number, subtract your current age and the difference will be the number of years you want to live well, healthy, and comfortably.

90 years old - ...... (your current age) = ... X .... (A) = ... (B)

This will represent the number of years, which you will multiply with the number we calculated earlier referred to as (A). This will give a whole new big number which will represent the total amount of money you will need to have in the bank so that you can live a financially free and comfortable life up to ninety years old. This number is referred to as (B). And that is your Magic Number. It gives you a sense of what level of wealth your life is currently aligned with, or you aspire to be aligned with.

Your role is to give everything you've got to make sure that this amount (B) is in the bank. Once you have that number, whatever you make on top of that will be everything you can use to give back, to help, and to contribute to causes you care about.

Therefore, the question is how many years do you need to make that number possible? How many years would you like to work hard and focused so that you can reach that amount while staying open to possibilities of attracting more wealth and abundance throughout?

This exercise is so powerful. It gives you the hint of what is possible. It starts putting the seed in your subconscious mind and letting it incubate. It will help you open your consciousness and tell yourself:

- What if you could make that a reality?
- What if you can become a match to abundance and wealth?
- What if you are a catalyst of wealth for you and for others?

Your Magic Number will bring you magic in your life when you are integrated in every part of your being. With your thoughts and strategic planning, with your emotional alignment, and with your attitude and actions.

"100 Million" Bond in the International Market

This year, as I was deepening my understanding of money energy, I pulled an award I received when I was at the World Bank Treasury from structuring and launching a hundred million bond. The World Bank Treasury is a trading room inside of the World Bank Institution. It's in charge of the management and the structuring of World Bank money from the international capital markets and financial systems. The World Bank raises funds in the international market by issuing bonds, ranked AAA for institutional investors to invest their money in for a specific rate depending on the length of the bond and the currency.

I was in charge of raising IBRD (World Bank) bonds in emerging market currencies. This meant opening new markets by being able to use their local currencies to raise funds in the international sphere. And the first one I worked on through the whole process was in Polish Zloty. "100 millions PNZ" was written big and clear on it. That is the equivalent of forty to fifty million USD at that time. I didn't make much of it then. It was normal and natural. All the development projects required money to become reality and money was out there. The role of the treasury was to create that link between institutional investors and local development. It was selling without selling. It's more informing with all the respect, the intellectual sophistication, and the humanness of the mission. The World Bank has been growing and growing around the mission of a World Free of Poverty and creating a sustainable future for everyone.

Going back to those moments, the World Bank Treasury was structured in a way that it was normal to handle this level of money because there's so much money out there, the spreadsheet will be filled at the right moment. Never was there any worry about whether there would be investors coming or not. The focus was about making the pitch so powerful and genuine, and all the rest would unfold. The emotional intelligence of the institution was at the highest vibe. Because there was a strong belief in the mission and it was all connected to making a difference in people's lives. Investors were driven by their deep interest to help humanity and to feel part of the process. It was all about human connections and the finances were unfolding naturally around them.

Using the business language, it was selling with a humanness side of it and financial sophistication. It was selling bonds without ever feeling like selling. Investors were so happy to find a great opportunity that they could invest in. These clients were happy to find the right fit for them and to grasp the opportunity. And the clear mission of the institution was focusing and excelling to do the development work, to create new projects, new impact, and make a difference in people's lives.

Mastering the Selling Process

Mastering the selling process is your mechanics to make your goals and financial objectives unfold. It comes naturally in alignment with who you are and what you do.

Actually, everything we do is about selling. So, in any conversation, you need to first be anchored in your context and your vision of things.

Then you need to be able to bring the person you are talking to to the level of excitement that you have.

Every conversation is actually a sales conversation. Discussing with your partner or with your friends. Talking with your children is selling to them your way of seeing what they should do and how they behave.

For example, when my five year old is jumping up and doing crazy things when it is beyond bedtime. If I go and ask her to go to bed, she will be shocked and upset. At that moment we are completely disconnected from each other. I'm in the space where I feel that she needs to be sleeping, and she is in a hyper mode. We aren't in the same zone. I need to bring her to my level of calmness by calming her down and helping her get in the emotional sync so that she can get ready to go to bed. Her excitement was way too high to get her to calm down. The same thing about selling. The excitement will then be at your level and you need to bring others to get ready so they can buy your product. It takes preparation and walking together until they meet you at the same level of excitement.

The interaction between you selling a thought, service, or a product needs to get you to an energetic alignment so that you can be in sync. It's about energy, feeling, and synchronizing the vibes.

When you align your energy with the frequency of clients ready and resourceful, clients happy with your service and your product, you will get yourself in the zone and invite them to join you there. It comes through your way of being.

Going back to putting my five year old to bed. My context around my children is to have the most beautiful and fruitful relationship for now, when they are young and when they become adults. That is what matters to me, so that when my daughter looks back to her childhood, she will be happy and feel lucky about her journey.

Which means that if it's just me with her, I will treat her with that context. I don't have to wait until I have people around me, or be in public to treat my child with respect and caring. Because someone is watching. I'm the same even when I'm by myself with them. This is what it means to have a consistent context, a consistent way of being, and consistent vibes. You're aligned with them no matter what. You don't alter them to better fit who is looking, or who is listening.

This goes with everything you do in your life and in your work. If you're selling a service or a product and you are presenting live, making a speech. The attitude you have at that moment when you know the world is watching should mirror the attitude you have when no one is looking. By honoring yourself in every part, by embodying the ideal person you want yourself to be in every part. By respecting others the way you respect yourself. By loving others the way you love yourself.

Remove any resistance that would come from negative and deprecating thoughts about yourself. We are thought to be rude to ourselves and to treat ourselves with names and badly at times. Sometimes, it's so mechanical, you don't even realize that you aren't treating yourself properly and that you're bringing yourself down in vibrations without feeling it.

Approach every conversation with love and respect, because you are co-creating. Therefore, selling is about being aligned in the same zone, bringing excitement to both sides by creating a genuine connection. By caring for the person, you are selling more than just adding more names on an Excel spreadsheet.

When you approach selling as an experience, it becomes exciting because it comes with all the fascination and its uniqueness as you discover the potential buyer. You give the space for it because you are creating a lasting relationship, you aren't just selling using manipulative tactics. You are selling with honor and respect for others. Just like the big designer brand you feel so happy buying from because you're treated as an important person by them. You feel a sense of belonging to a category of high-level lifestyle. The designer brands aren't focusing on convincing you to buy or tricking you to buy; they focus on providing world class products and service. The model is based on building a long-term relationship with your clients and connections. And it works. Because one transaction is not ripe to happen today, it will happen when the timing is right from the other side. When you provide an open space, perseverance and consistency will make its way to you.

This is why the focus should be about deepening your knowledge and your excellence in what you do. So that you show up always improved, grown, and with something new. As soon as you finish a presentation, you will feel grown up and improved.

This way people will know that there is always something new, improved, and excellent. Because you have chosen excellence as your brand and excellence comes in every facet of your business. When people are excited about something it means that you have somehow triggered their curiosity. And when you do that, you create a mutual excitement and expectations which will feel aligned when your offer is the best of you. And your offer is the best of you, when you care for your clients and for others.

When you create the excitement and curiosity, you start getting your clients aligned with what you have and who you are. The selling becomes normal and natural. In the entertainment world, movies gross billions of dollars in the box office just by their announcements. The curiosity arouses the excitement, and on the day of release everyone wants to be the first one to see it. The industry is based on excitement, curiosity, and connection with people. People will go and buy without knowing much about the movie, just the title, the actor, or maybe a photo from one scene. Sometimes without anything, just catchy music. They create the experience of excitement for the buyers, which makes it the best selling experience.

When it comes to selling your product or your offer, you have to create the whole context around you, so that you vibe completely with it and you invite your clients and buyers to join you in the world that you have created. If you want the experience to make them feel good, create a surrounding around you of feeling good, elegant, and safe.

Being in the women empowerment sphere, it is all about making women feel valued, elegant, beautiful, and respected. That's how I treat everyone I meet whether I am selling or simply connecting. The same vibes, the same feeling, and the same energy. Because selling is for me through the money, is for you through the knowledge and the under-standing you get, and for us through the transformation we will be creating together for both of us. As my clients grow, I grow with them. I mature, I understand more, and I become a better mentor, a better strategist, and a better mindset and business coach.

So be honest about the excitement you create, as you build a genuine connection and be truly caring. It starts by stimulating curiosity and building the connection. Selling is about emotions and humanness. It has to come from within you, it isn't about copying what others are doing and showing up. Something will be off because each one is unique. And your uniqueness is that perfection in you. Find your story as it aligns with who you are and connect with the why behind all that you do.

Henceforth, by focusing on the best experience for the buyer and the best service to your client, it will all unfold. Any strategy you use will work when you try it and improve it by doing. Some strategies work for someone, but maybe not for you. Take what makes you feel that you are moving forward but adapt to what vibes with you. You can niche down when you are looking to sell to make it tight. You can also choose to broaden your outlook to integrate many groups if you have the ability to hold several stories at the same time and switch from one to another. There are business strategies that prove to be successful for some parts of business and not for others. What we know for sure is that by doing and repeating over and over, you can set up your own trend.

Start by adopting a strategy while trusting your own capacity to find the best that fits your uniqueness. Nothing happens overnight. It takes work and consistency. This is why it's important to embody a life that vibes forward. Any small step, be grateful for it and carry on. We often underestimate what we can do in a year when we are consistent. You will grow, evolve, and rise wiser and with experience that makes you ready to give back and serve.

Finally, selling is caring about people and about making their life better. It starts with building a genuine connection and standing with credibility and expertise. It's about holding the space for your clients and being continuously aligned to your vision. When focusing on the excellence in your work and the service you offer, recognition will come and money will follow.

When you do something that is meaningful and impactful, even those who didn't like you will start finding the good in what you do. Carry on in the same road and have faith about reaching your beautiful destination. Success is the journey; walk that journey with a foot grounded in gratitude and a foot towards your desire and aspiration.

My Workbook - Chapter 6

Calculate My Magic Number

Make a list of all your expenses:

- Housing _____
- Electricity, water, gas_____
- Car_____
- Groceries _____
- School _____
- Health_____
- Hobbies_____
- Traveling _____
- Feeling good _____
- Extras_____

= Total _____ X 12 months

=_____(A)

My age =

I want to live well, healthy, and financially comfortable up to = 90 years old

How many years

90 - _____ =.   X .... (A) =_____ (M)

   (my age)   yearly need

(M) is my Magic number

How many years do I want to work hard for = _____(B)_

How much will I make per year to hit my Magic Number =

7

Create Wealth and Make an Impact

You need money to make an impact.

You need money to travel to go help the people you want to help. You need money to have the team to structure the projects and the initiatives so that you can create more impact. You need money to inform the people you are helping about your existence and the service you do. So to make an impact, you actually need to create wealth for you and for all the others that you're helping by your incredible dedication to development.

The first reaction I always get from women when I talk about creating wealth is how they're not interested in making money, all they want is to help people and make an impact. Why are these two aspects kept separate? How can you help when you don't help yourself?

I see women creating associations and communities to help women, children, or the planet, and struggling to make ends meet and feeling that's the way it is. For any work or help to be sustainable, it has to balance itself. The only way to do that is by creating the financial flows to hold your vision, your heart-centered mission, and the impact you want to make.

Kamar came to the Mastermind looking for her calling. After working together, she got all the boosts and clarified what she wanted to do. As a pianist and a musician, she wanted to create an association to be able to help handicapped children or children with special needs have access to music lessons and playing piano. The whole project is about helping. But to be able to help she needs the money to rent or buy the space, and to market her work to let parents of children with special needs know about the incredible work she is doing. All of this needs financing. In addition, the business has to balance itself so that it offers a stable cash-flow for Kamar to feel financially free and give all her focus to helping more children.

The same thing with France-based Zahra, a high-level university math professor, affiliated to the most distinguished research center in France the CNRSS. Preparing for her retirement, Zahra needed help articulating her next focus. It was about helping young girls access math and STEM. Such a noble cause starts with wealth creation so that the impact can be real and sustainable. Yes, there are sponsors and donors, but it all starts by your openness and readiness to attract and receive wealth. Otherwise, you will be blocking it yourself before it even comes.

So creating wealth and attracting money is for you, and for everyone you're destined to help grow and improve in whatever form you choose to call your mission. In my work today, creating wealth as I grow my business, I openly and deeply feel that it is for me, for you, and for us together. It is for me as I sell additional programs. It's for you as you get to experience the most profound, complete, and holistic transformation, attracting more money into your life and returning your investment right away. And it's for us, because we will grow as we increase the wealth around us. We get to experience more magical things in our life and we get to help more people around us. The ripple effect of the impact is like a wave that spreads around.

We grow together when we have the means for it. And the means for it comes with the money you have and the abundance you attract in your life.

This chapter is to articulate those interlinkages between wealth creation, abundance, and making a sustainable impact.

It Starts by Finding Your *Why*

Take a moment to remember the why behind everything you do and everything you think about.

Why are you getting up every day? Why are you seeking excellence? Why are you continuously trying to be better? Why are you looking for ways to stand out? Why deep inside of you do you believe in yourself?

When you answer these questions, it opens up your consciousness and helps you find your deep calling. What is the drive in you that makes you carry on and help you set up the context for you? When you have a clear vision, you will create a whole set up about how you see it and how you will be in it. So find that spark in you. When you do, let it grow and guide you.

I did this over and over each time I was faced with challenges in my professional life and had to recreate myself!

I remembered the *why* behind my working hard. The *why* behind the long nights I spent studying to be at the top of the class in math and physics. I would wake up and leave my bed while my sister was sleeping to sit outside of my room in the corridor to work on my lessons. It took a lot of strong will to do that and an anchored belief that I would go high with those studies, I would go far with these learnings.

That same feeling kept me going when I spent long nights at Harvard University finalizing a report or a study or a research paper. The same thing when I started working. Long days and weekends at the World Bank preparing high-level meetings and faraway missions. I sat in so many long meetings. I spent so many long hours at my desk writing, presenting, analyzing, understanding, and coordinating.

In retrospect, what kept me going when I felt overwhelmed, when I felt it was too much, was my deep belief in my mission. I embraced the role I have prepared for all these years. I was in the center of all the work at the institutional level and the national level. The objective was vivid and present to reach sustainable development and make a difference in people's life.

I studied, researched, and worked about how to create portfolios of projects that make an organization lead the way in terms of sustainability. This applied to both the private and the public sector. Because development calls for the mobilization of all the stakeholders, it's finding the harmony between them and making sure that everyone integrates sustainability in what they do.

Two years ago, I had a calling to become a catalyst for women's empowerment and leadership. So my mission today is about making a real impact directly on women. It's how to restore gender equality around leadership, wealth creation, and making a sustainable impact. Because gender equality is at the root of every facet of sustainability. This is how we can create sustainable futures!

When you find your *why*, it becomes your deeply rooted identity. It's unique to you and is a way to let your spiritual perfection shine. Make your why so big that it overwhelms you and drives you far!

Your why is also related to your real story. To how you grew up, your traditions, your culture, your background. It's related to everything you experienced in your life, good and tough. They shaped the amazing person you are today, the incredible personality you have grown up to have. And they created the true identity you have in you. If you've grasped everything in chapter three, you will know how to go beyond the voices in your head that aren't cheering you up to dig inside for the diamond in you.

Because in each one of you, there is a perfect diamond. So unique, so special, so you. And that perfect diamond was covered through the years with multiple layers. These layers are all the frustrations, the difficulties. The many times you heard "no, you can't," the many times you weren't praised when you were expecting it or needing it. All of the times you looked at what others were doing and felt you deserved it. The multiple occasions you felt anger, rage for someone who mistreated you and hurt you. The times you let jealousy overwhelm you watching the luxurious display of the life of a much younger generation with less credentials and knowledge. These layers cover the perfect diamond in you.

So what do you do to show up fresh and polished? You put on nail polish to cover all those layers. You go to meetings dressed the part, you make important conversation. You show up and do the work. But something is missing, something is not quite aligned. Because in reality, what you need to do is to remove all these layers one after the other. Remove all the negative energies that cover your intuitive side and your perfect diamond. When you do that, you will be radiating the light like how a diamond reflects the light and magnetizes everyone around.

At that moment, you will know that you have reached your deepest why and you will use your story to rise and to reach a higher level of success, of wins, of celebrations. The impact will come as a natural consequence.

Find the Trigger of Your Story

Being an engineer, my mind has always been structured differently. I learned early on how to bring everything back to numbers and to science. This means that my brain is always making calculations and finding logic in different situations. When I go shopping, I calculate everything—the budget, the total, the spending. So I find myself like a walking calculator. It doesn't bother me, but I am continuously stimulated with numbers. It has also been a way for me to feel alert all the time.

Today, I use that to help women structure their business plan and their professional life so that they can own their space completely. Numbers and finance can be impressive and overwhelming, but in reality all you need to be on top of your business is the basic arithmetic you need when you go grocery shopping. It's the repetition and the ease with numbers that makes it possible. Also, your familiarity with different levels of calculation makes you feel comfortable around big wealth.

The very fact that I started in development made being around hundred of millions of dollars a normal business day. I was part of projects with nine figures and I was structuring and working to raise global bonds which are around one billion USD for World Bank development projects. That level of money felt normal because development requires billions and trillions of investments. However, I could only connect that with large institutions and structures. Because contributing to development meant handling and structuring large projects and initiatives to alleviate poverty, for basic infrastructure and capacity building. This mission is so broad it calls for a very high level of wealth and money. This meant structuring, evaluating, and analyzing projects were around nine figures and more. National level strategies, regional initiatives, take so much investment and true impact.

For that large part of my career, it was about giving my all and contributing to every initiative I was part of and every project I was privileged to be part of incredible development changes. New water infrastructure projects, large renewable energy power plants. New policies and action plans at the national level, regional level, and local level. It was incredible. The impact and the satisfaction that came from it was profound. It made me feel happy, useful, and in my element. I was prepared for it, trained for it, and had my mindset through so many years that it felt natural. I was owning the space and understanding development from the deepest part of my heart. I was coming from the developing world and had traveled the world, so it was concrete and real. I spoke from my heart and felt connected. This was how I experienced my professional career as a journey of discovery, evolution, personal growth, and true impact.

When I became an entrepreneur, I approached my work from the perspective of service and helping. Yet the money part needed some adjustment. It was only after making money and losing money that I started to understand my own money paradigm. I had to go through my own elevation and healing to better serve as I redefined my own mission. It was no longer about general development, but it was about people, women, and direct impact. I reshaped my mission to empower women so that they could lead themselves to wealth, joy, happiness, fulfillment, and peace of mind.

Women are at the center of every development, every change, and every improvement. When you invest in women, you can have a lasting impact. When you empower women, you create gender equality in different levels of society and industries. And gender equality crosses all the sustainable development goals. It's at the root of sustainable economies and businesses.

I see the impact at the human level. The ripple effect will help compound all these efforts and create a world where young girls and young women feel empowered by growing confident, resilient, tech savvy, and financially free.

It Started With How "Every Living Thing Is Made from Water"

In my journey as a leader in sustainability, finance, and development, it started from water and the deep meaning of water. When I joined the World Bank, the first advice that was given to me was that for anyone to go up the corporate ladder fast, I had to be a recognized expert in one field and know all the other fields because managers need to be able to lead different specialists at the same time. It was about playing full in a team and focusing on one field. At that moment, I was focusing on water because my professor, mentor, and PhD adviser was Prof. Peter Rogers, an international reference in water management. I developed that deep connection with water, and my whole world started to revolve around it.

Water is the source of life. Old civilizations settled down around sources of water. Nomads traveled hundreds of kilometers searching for water, and animals migrate looking for water.

Water is the source of joy and happiness. Communities thrive when it rains, and agriculture develops around water availability. Similarly for industries and urbanization. Growth and acceleration were synchronized around smart and optimized water management, and the integration of new sources of water including recycling, desalination, and many others.

Water is the source of creativity and inspiration. Painters, musicians, and writers used water to get inspired. In other spheres, innovators and business owners are making billions around water, from logistics, production, fisheries, and boating. An incredible evolution is helping reach a whole new dimension of the blue economy. There's such a power in understanding the role of nature around you. And water, in particular, is central to it all.

I studied water for many years at Harvard University with my dear Professor Peter Rogers. And my PhD thesis was about integrating water management into national planning. Being an engineer and studying economics, I connected the engineering part of water to the larger picture of national planning and integrated economic development. So everything I studied, read, analyzed, and worked on was around water for many years. Then I added to it renewable energies with the rise of solar and wind energies. Additionally, I was growing and getting further into a position to hold more in my mission and my broader context.

I was also very aware of the importance of sustainability as I had studied and mastered every aspect of it. Consequently, I could stand and use my voice to speak for how sustainability isn't a choice anymore, it's a must today. We cannot talk about business development or business growth without looking at the impact water has. And the impact is considered from an economic, social, and environmental perspective. Therefore, every business and person has a role to play in getting closer to the Global Sustainable Goals depending on their industry and the sector where they operate. This means that whatever you do when it comes from a space of helping and serving gets aligned with the needs for sustainable development.

It helped me keep a larger perspective from an early age by understanding where my work, research, and later all of my business fit in the global sphere. I kept my vision broad and alive.

This is how I kept my objectives and my mission so big it was hard to let go of them. The impact was the underlying essence. This was seen as my whole context. It was so meaningful, with so much to be done and so many miles to cross. Within this context, all the objectives were very important; they helped me change my path when things didn't work out.

This way, all the hurdles and the obstacles were part of the journey. I kept going, discovering new ways to redefine my mission. I kept going, rewriting my objectives to better fit my passion for development and women's empowerment.

And my objective of this book and this last chapter in particular is to leave you with a clear understanding about the central role to play in making a better future and leaving a legacy behind.

When you frame your goal with a broader mission, it becomes a bigger journey. You will feel it getting intertwined with your everyday life, and find a naturally motivating boost from your noble cause. This is how you'll overcome deception and difficulties by remembering your calling.

When you embody the broad mission, the impact will be in every corner of your work. This way the path to get there becomes an ongoing discovery. A process with increasing progress and celebrations.

This is the walk for success that you will be able to master at this stage. Place one foot in gratitude for what you have created and achieved, and one foot in the desire to get closer to your objectives.

My objective today is to help women become great leaders by creating wealth and making an impact.

Keep a Large-Scale Perspective

You can see making an impact as small or as big as you want. You can keep your perspective boxed by what is surrounding you and get into pitiful comparison with your peers, siblings, and neighbors. This will keep you small, as if you were limited by the size of a village. Or you can broaden your consciousness, use technology and feel how you are connected to two billion people from all around the world through a click. It gives you a bigger perspective and helps you anchor your imagination. Imagination doesn't have any limit, we choose to block it by our own beliefs. When you become aware of those blockages, it carries you very far beyond all limitations.

I met a very smart lady, Dina, who wanted to create a program to empower women through training. We started our work structuring the program together, but while defining it, we worked on the mindset and felt comfortable about structuring a national level of programs. It took us two months of mindset work and strategy, before being able to define and start negotiating a two-point-five million USD contract. The impact wasn't only bigger but the scale-up made it more in line with the client's needs. Sometimes you have to go big to make it look plausible and aligned with your target and the impact you want to truly make. That means that you have to become energetically a match to that level of numbers and money.

You don't need to be an established entrepreneur or a wiz to structure six and seven figure programs. It takes a good idea about something you really love doing, a strong belief in it, a structured plan, and of course the will to do it. Because all you need is the ability to see the big picture.

Once you clarify your objective and find the gap in your market to fit your unique offer, then you can structure your project or company by identifying the impact you want to make and calculating the financial goal. Then you reverse engineer the perfect strategic plan to create a model to help you achieve your aspiration.

It's about planning, strategy, and most importantly having a strong mindset of success with a clean alignment with your context for you to get the right vibes.

During my twenty years in strategy and finance, what I have excelled in doing is structuring large-scale initiatives and turning them into reality from the financial, operational, and accountability aspects.

Therefore, if your dream is to create your own stage and to launch a seven figures program or beyond, make it happen. Just like Dina structured her two-point-five million USD program to empower women and contribute to improving gender equality at a local and national level. Also, how Fadwa attracted a one million USD investment in her startup in the clean energy sector, by structuring all the financial parts and owning her business model and becoming energetically aligned with that level of wealth.

So, what will be your crazy, big dream project? Don't shy away from it.

I used to think that you needed to be a well-established international institution to embark on a large-scale global mission. Until I listened to my calling and decided to make women's empowerment my mission. I had that spark of insight one day coming back home after a tumultuous day at work. I looked at my three girls and decided to power up for them and for every girl on the planet.

This is why creating your stage is up to you. And launching a big program starts with you making the firm decision to make a real impact around you. To know that you are making a difference in someone's life. It could just be by bringing a smile, or offering a product or a service he or she needs.

What is helping me carry on is the gratitude for every step I'm taking. The gratitude for all the changes and impact on the lives of dozens and dozens of women from all over the world. Growing more confident, more aware of their possibilities, and more empowered to take on their life and go after their dream job or create and scale up their dream enterprise.

To express this gratitude, we celebrate every day the big leaps women are making through the BAL Method. They become true role models for many women and young girls looking for guidance and inspiration. This way, the impact becomes universal!

Find a Way to Serve

When you focus on serving and on helping, you are embodying the true understanding of making an impact around you. Because service is what stays.

People are more interested in becoming famous, a star, or an influencer. Women are often looking for what they want because they don't know what they need to get there. The world doesn't need one more Youtuber or TikToker with perfect lipstick and dresses. The world needs true inspiration with real contribution. A way of improving someone's life by providing a skill or a knowledge so that they can also reach their dream.

You can become the most inspiring and known influencer through the work you provide, the service you do so that you can help humanity thrive. It could be by creating a product we need to make our life better, by teaching a lesson or technique you learn to improve the smallest part of people's way of being.

Martin Luther King Jr. said, "Not everybody can be famous but everybody can be great, because greatness is determined by service."

Choose to be great by providing the best service you can. In this digital era, your greatness will make you famous, you will make yourself stand out as the go-to expert. When you get into a deep understanding of service and your paradigm becomes overwhelmed by service, you will be in true alignment with the significance of what you are doing. That alignment is your inner force, connecting you from within through your own vibration and to the outside world with the impact you make happen. You radiate fully in harmony with what is the highest form of fulfillment. You will feel content, satisfied, and fulfilled.

Looking at the most successful people in the world, I realized they all embody serving at the highest level of its meaning. Whether it was in terms of new creations such as Elon Musk with Tesla, or Bill Gates with software like Microsoft, or Jennifer Lopez through songs. Different ways, different sectors. What they have in common is serving humanity, and truly believing in their mission.

This is why when you focus on serving, you will reach the highest form of your inner vibration and as it relates to the impact you want to give.

What brings the highest form of fulfillment is having a true impact around you. As small as saying a hello with a smile to someone, to being instrumental in improving someone's life by bringing her or him hope, inspiration, a new skill, or a new something she or he wanted or needed.

It's a way to give back to the world. When you bring excellence to it, you honor yourself. In addition, when you find the significance in what you do, it makes you feel that inner alignment we all thrive for. Which feels like peace of mind with a beautiful harmony. Excellence makes you stand out and be appreciated. Alignment comes from filling up your inner force of life with fulfillment, love, and significance.

When you start with excellence, significance, fulfillment, and success will come. This is why you must focus on providing the best service using your multicultural background, experience, credentials, and knowledge.Provide a service from your heart and with all the caring. This is the type of service that will help you make a lasting impact and create incredible abundance and overflowing wealth.

Spiritual beings having a human experience every step of the way. Be incredibly happy for every minute, every hour, for every day, so that you can turn your life into a joyful and sweet experience. It will strengthen your inner spirit and create a shield around you to feel protected when times are tough. And trust the process. Trust is faith and belief without evidence.

I love what Oprah said answering the "who am I?" question. In her own words: "I want to fulfill the highest, truest expression of myself as a human being. I want to fulfill the promise that the creator dreamed when he dreamed the cells that made up me." Her motivation is not driven by the usefulness of the work she does, of leaving a legacy behind.

When I think about it, to me, this started to resonate when I understood what it means to celebrate every part of your life, the good events and the setbacks, the achievements and the challenges, the joy and the hurt. All of it makes the beauty of life.

Understand what it means to celebrate the spiritual perfection you have inside of you. It makes you grow. It makes you elevate. You start connecting your soul to the infinite possibilities.

The Power of Love

It's all about "I love you" as how you say it and connect with it to yourself, to others, and how you receive it.

Saying "I love you" to yourself truly with the emotional connection will transform your life. Louise Hay based all of her transformational work on the importance of loving yourself. The most important relationship that you have is the one with yourself because that relationship will never leave you. It is a lasting one. There's a simple exercise you can do to start raising your awareness about your worthiness. Saying "I love you" will help you regain consideration for yourself and start getting aligned with the vibes of gratitude. It will not happen overnight and you need to keep on doing it until you witness the change. Because, when you are in the lowest phase of your life, loving yourself every day a tiny bit more is the only way you can start raising your vibration. One of the lowest vibrations you can be at is the shame of who you are and when you feel a deep unworthiness with a depressing state of mind.

It's like leading yourself or others. It isn't something that will happen in a day. It's small actions that you do consistently every day. So be nice to yourself like you are nice to others. Honor yourself and be proud of every part of you. This is how you can raise your worthiness and your value.

The second layer is about finding the courage to transform your life, to improve your sense of safety, and create that environment where you feel that everything is going to be okay.

Finding the courage is never from the inside. You don't look for it inside of you or go for a ten-day secluded meditation and come back with courage. No. Courage is external. You need to find it on the outside.

Our courage comes from the support we feel from others. That feeling you get when someone around you has your back. And when you know that if you can't do it, someone is there to tell you "I got you" or "you will be okay."

That's what gives you the courage to do what you do and to carry on and recreate yourself after problems and struggles. Those relationships that we foster are the ones that feed us the courage we need in our lives. And when you find the courage to move ahead, to carry on, you become an inspiration to others and you will give the courage to someone else.

We are social animals, and it's important for us to develop and foster true relationships. Because we draw our courage from that love. When someone around you can truly tell you, "I love you," it can save your life. It can save you from giving up. It can also save you from negative thoughts, depression, and from losing yourself.

Having the love and the courage makes leaders that have not only the human side but can inspire others, and will always do the right thing no matter what.

Becoming a leader isn't something that you will transform into overnight. It takes discipline and consistency. Discipline is about being consistent in leading yourself to whom you want to become. When you feel yourself with love and caring about yourself, and you are able to lead yourself, you will be prepared to lead others by your way of being.

Being a good leader is when you do the work with excellence and you serve with significance. And being a great leader is when you truly care for the people around you. It's when you add humanness to the work you do that you become a great leader.

The best test for a good leader is when you ask someone how he's doing and actually care about the answer. When you are an executive and you have several people working for you, you probably cannot care and connect with everyone, but you can spread the vibes about caring throughout the organization.

The best example of great leadership comes from parenthood. Parents want the best for their children. They invest in them and they care for their success. They help them build their self-confidence so they can achieve something bigger than their parents could do. That's the leadership we are talking about that brings greatness, humanness, excellence, and alignment.

With Love Always, Gratitude, Light, and Power

Live your life to the fullest.

Be happy, be sad, be grateful for every step.

Don't wait and don't hold back.

Don't ever give up.

Trust the universe and the divine.

It is a continuous process to see harmony unfolding in your life.

Believe in yourself and in the possibilities.

Act on it by using your genius and making excellence your brand.

And lead yourself to a great life of service and sustainable impact!

I love you.

You are beautiful.

You are powerful.

You are glorious.

You are strong.

And if you have to go through difficult things for you to see it, so be it!

Go forth and have the most exciting life!

My Workbook - Chapter 7

What is my vision for a better world?

How can I serve through my work and my professional role?

What will be the message I want to share today with the world?

Gratitude

Thank you for taking the time to read this book and understanding the essence of the Believe-Act-Lead Method.

This book is dedicated to every woman who wants to stand out by making a difference around her through her work, art, creativity, vision, and leadership.

If you received any benefit from reading this book, please pass it on so that someone else can also benefit from it.

I would love you to leave a review of this book on Goodreads.com or on Amazon at https://amzn.to/3D4RTe4.

This is a push to inspire you, to bring you some positive vibes so that you can continue your own leadership journey to happiness, success, peace of mind, and financial freedom.

Make the BAL Method your own and use it to lead yourself to greatness and to make the world a better place for all of us.

Acknowledgments

Every day, I am so honored to have been in the midst of incredible women who participated in the Empowered Leaders Mastermind and who powered up and transformed from deep inside with the BAL Method (Believe-Act-Lead Method). Both in the English, French, and Arabic program, I want to acknowledge every woman, and also the few men, who joined.

I have so much gratitude and love for all these women who trusted me as their guide and who followed the process with so much dedication, discipline, and loyalty. I would like to acknowledge all of you ladies. Some of them I shared their inspiring stories in the book, because as they were powering up, and growing through their own transformation week after week, feeling the magic in their life, celebrating incredible wins as the sessions went by, I was getting empowered myself. I was growing better and better in the delivery of my work, in the way I was showing up, and in the pursuit of my incredible mission.

This book is for all of you. For all the pain and hurt, the struggles and difficulties, the setbacks and bumps in the road ... they only show you that you're stronger than all of it. They show you how you can illuminate your glow, allow it to guide you to your most beautiful destination, and experience a journey of success, joy, happiness, and peace of mind. I created the BAL Method for every woman so that she can celebrate herself, her life, her genius, her power and let her unique and precious diamond shine.

You are such amazing women and so special. There is incredible magic surrounding us and for you to tap into. This all brought so much sense to my life again, after a big professional challenge. Today, I truly believe that every challenge comes with an extraordinary opportunity. And that opportunity for me is this. I discovered the most precious service of teaching the BAL Method to every woman. My vision is to create a world where every young girl and young woman can grow confident, resilient, tech savvy, and financially free.

A special thank you to Red Thread Publishing, and particularly to Sierra Melcher, Adrienne MacIain, and Marian (Mimi) Rich.

For me,

For my son and my three daughters,

For you ladies,

And for all of us!

About the Author

Dr. Hynd Bouhia has accumulated more than 25 years of professional experience in high-level leadership positions in strategy and finance. She was nominated by Forbes among the 100 most influential women and most influential Arab women in Business (2015), and honored as a member of the Johns Hopkins Society of Scholars (2018).

With a Harvard PhD in environmental engineering and sustainable development, and an Engineering degree from Centrale Paris, Dr. Hynd started her career at the World Bank in Washington working on development projects and infrastructure. She then joined Morocco's Prime

Minister as an economic advisor where she worked on the elaboration of Morocco's industrial strategies and the structuring of large scale investment projects in industry, energy, and tourism. Dr. Hynd was appointed the Managing Director of the Casablanca Stock Exchange, and structured and managed several investment funds before launching the consulting firm Strategica specialized in economic intelligence and impact entrepreneurship.

Dr. Hynd is the author of two inspirational and women empowerment books *African Girl, African Woman: How agile, empowered and tech-savvy females will transform the continent... for good,* and the French book, *Filles et Femmes de l'Afrique Moderne: Comment deviennent-elles leaders du continent.*

Dr. Hynd is the founder of the BAL Method and Femme LEADER to empower women from around the world by teaching them impact entrepreneurship and how to become a great leader by creating wealth and making an impact. She is on a mission to empower a billion girls and women around the world to grow confident, resilient, tech-savvy, and financially free, by using her BAL Method, so that every girl and every woman embraces her dream and assertively *Believe in It. Act on It. Lead with It.*

https://linktr.ee/hyndbouhia

Register here for the BAL newsletter:

www.balmethod.com/materclass

Get the BAL Digital Course of 10 modules and more than 60 lessons in english and 60 lessons in french :

www.balmethod.com/digital

About the Publisher

Red Thread Publishing Group

Red Thread Publishing is an all-female publishing company on a mission to support 10,000 women to become successful published authors and thought leaders. Through the transformative work of writing & telling our stories we are not only changed as individuals, but we are also changing the global narrative & thus the world.

Visit us at:

www.redthreadbooks.com

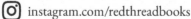 facebook.com/redthreadpublishing
instagram.com/redthreadbooks

Also by Dr. Hynd Bouhia

https://www.amazon.com/Hynd-Bouhia/e/B001HPH8G6

African Girl, African Woman: How agile, empowered and tech-savvy females will transform the continent... for good

Filles et femmes de l'Afrique Moderne: Comment deviennent-elles des leaders du continent

Water in the Macro Economy: Integrating economics and engineering into a n Analytical Model (Ashgate Studies in Environmental and Natural resources Economics)

Coming Soon

The Codes of Self-Leadership